T0078003

Listen: you will hear the music

Elizabeth J. Shaw

WESTBOW
PRESS®
A DIVISION OF THOMAS NELSON
& ZONDERVAN

WestBow Press books may be ordered through booksellers or by contacting:

WestBow Press
A Division of Thomas Nelson & Zondervan
1663 Liberty Drive
Bloomington, IN 47403
www.westbowpress.com
844-714-3454

ISBN: 978-1-9736-7745-1 (sc)
ISBN: 978-1-9736-7744-4 (e)

Print information available on the last page.

WestBow Press rev. date: 10/30/2020

I can do all things through Christ who gives me strength.
—Philippians 4:13, BSB

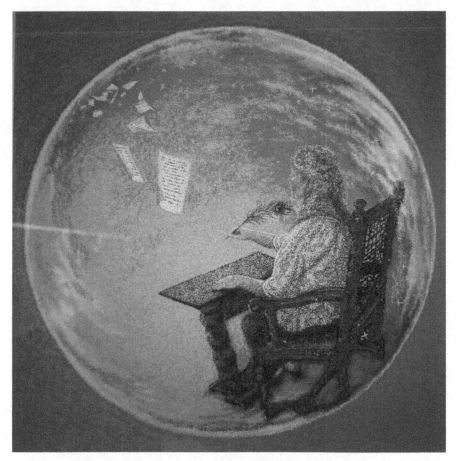

Vision God gave me when the book first started, page by page, inspiration by inspiration; story one after the other all for His glory. Thank you Father!

Credits to the artist Nikola Y. Z.

Dedications

Don't be selfish; don't try to impress others. Be humble,
thinking of others as better than yourselves.
Don't look out only for your own interests,
but take an interest in others, too.
—Philippians 2:3-4, NLT

Lord, you know, but I shall say it: You did it! I am convinced that by Your grace and inspiration this book became a reality.

To my husband without whom I would only be one half of a whole, you are my hero! Thank you for everything, dearest. You are a spiritual blessing; your invaluable support is truly appreciated. Praying and loving you softly.

To my daughter, a well-deserved "Thank you", for being supportive and extremely helpful every single day you are our gift from heaven. I appreciate you more and more each day, you'll remain in my heart forever—my sweet and graceful butterfly.

To my parents and my aunts, I love you. Dad, Mom, you are the past and present of these pages. Your tears prompted me to write.

Listen, Daddy! I am finally telling the world!

My friend and editor E.G., your faith and understanding were essential for the entirety of this book. I am filled with gratitude.

A big "Thank You" to Helen, your assistance was valuable and unexpected but greatly appreciated.

To my cousin Ivona P. S. and my acquaintance Nikola J. Z. both talented, great artists who drew two masterpieces I knew I had to include in this book. I am indebted to both of you for the amazing work you did.

West Bow Press: Brian Fox-PC, Carlos Cortes-ACR, Keith at the ALC, Joe Anderson-CIC, Carolyn N. Lockridge-PSA, Peter Le-MC, Juvy Luzon-Con., Bob De Groff-PSA: Thank you for your guidance and support.

To all who will work and assist in the process until this book goes to print and becomes a movie afterwards: "Thank you" from the bottom of my heart.

Contents

Contents

Prologue

Peace I leave with you; my peace I give you. I do not give to you as the world gives. Do not let your hearts be troubled and do not be afraid.
—John 14:27, NIV

Please stop for a moment. Place your belongings away and sit down. Don't you need to put your feet up? Make yourself comfortable, close your eyes, relax and enjoy the sound of the wind. Listen to its music, it softly swooshes playing with the leaves but most significantly it blends with the voice of the Lord. Be patient and attentive now. God never yells He speaks softly but distinctly. He speaks with authority. When we listen carefully, we can hear Him. If He calls on us, in order to distinguish Him from the evil one, we should rely on the message itself, for the Holy Spirit will reveal the truth and separate it from the lie. Throughout the course of history, God spoke to Adam, Eve, Noah, Job, Jacob, David, Solomon, Elijah, Isaiah, Jonah, Hosea, Zechariah, Moses, and so it goes. You and I may be next.

What makes us listen?

When we trust someone, we listen. In my experience I have heard You, Father, many times; and I knew it was—You. I did test the spirits. I made sure I asked more than once. Then, you assured me. I also realized I needed to stop what I was doing. You always told me important and amazing things. One time You advised me; the next time You softly reminded me; the third time You woke me up to give me the news . . . I can't recall how many times we had an encounter, but I know it was always something significant. An hour ago I spoke with a dear friend. She reminded me how her life had changed the day I told her You prompted me to help her. Father, You change lives, and You use us to be the carriers of good news. All we need to do is listen to you and obey.

The day I sat down to write the first pages of this book, it was You who spoke, and I kept writing. In less than a few hours, the first story was finished. I was on fire! I paid attention, and it all came so easily and flawlessly.

Whether You speak or act, it is always an incredible experience!

I have gained a lot spiritually and emotionally from interacting with You. Always caring, loving, and concerned, You have one agenda—to make us better people and use us to help others.

We live our lives convinced what we do is right. Some of us choose to live alongside You. Some choose to ignore Your existence and serve their ambitions, goals, and dark desires. You do not push, nor twist arms. You let us be, but You raise red flags along the way to warn us. You place knowledge and people reminding us one way or another, that there is a God. The rest is up to us.

I have disobeyed and seen how my life was nearly ruined when I strayed. Nothing can substitute for Your presence and guidance. Every encounter with You—moments I had, have now, and will have in the future—is priceless. I would not trade any of those amazing encounters for the biggest treasure on Earth.

The longer I walk with You, the more I realize how wonderful it all is. Many times, I am rushing, but You pull me back and let me see that rushing is useless. If I'm to expect a break through, I must rely on Your wisdom and leadership. You teach me how to do things and when to do them plus why I should or I shouldn't, as a result I become secure, more confident, and trustworthy. Then, I am capable of achieving more than I have imagined. You tell us that when You establish us among others, and we are "faithful over a little," then You "will set [us] over much" in order to further Your kingdom (Matthew 25:23, ESV).

Thank You for the book, for the learning experiences along the way, for teaching me patience and showing me that listening can be extremely important, for making my life richer, and, last but not least, for using me to be Your spokesperson.

1

What Does It Mean—I Can Do All Things Through Christ?

(cf: Philippians 4:13)

And he said unto me, My grace is sufficient for thee:
for my strength is made perfect in weakness.
— 2 Corinthians 12:9a, KJV

2016 was a year that brought a lot of questions and uncertainties into my life. I was stumbling and wondering why there is stillness and quietness. My direct line to Jesus was busy. Maybe the Lord had changed his phone number. Like a leaf drying in the autumn sun and slowly falling towards the ground, my faith was fading. I was becoming empty and hollow. My senses were dull, and my Christ was so far from my heart. I was asking the Lord whether he had put me on trial to test my faith and find whether I was worthy. Moments of doubt crept into my thoughts, and I was lonelier than ever. My daughter is one of my confidants, but now was not the time to let her know that I was struggling with doubts and precariousness. What kind of an example was I going to set for her? Her still fragile faith was not grounds for shaking. So, I kept the secret deep in my soul and set on this journey alone. My husband and I agree to disagree about faith; he expresses his love for God in a way that is different from mine. I am grateful that he loves the Lord and has given his life to Jesus!

As the year ended and 2017 showed a lot of promise, I was slowly coming out of this pit. My children's ministry at church was growing, and my sky was clearing as the thundering clouds were blown slowly away by winds of trust. God knew the future, and he was molding me, making me stronger—more dependent on Him. Trusting Him blindly was what He wanted me to learn. This precursor of what came next was very helpful, although no one is prepared to face adversity.

In November of 2017, out of the blue, my husband was diagnosed with a rare melanoma eye cancer. This was a punch in the face I was not ready for. His condition was calling for immediate action, and one of the best surgical specialists in the country performed the surgery in a matter of weeks. He was in the hospital for an entire week. His eye was taken out, and a special device was placed behind the eye that blasted the tumor with strong radiation. During this time he was in excruciating pain. At the end of the week, his eye was taken out again and the device removed. I was with him the day of the surgery and remained by his hospital bed the entire day, not realizing that I exposed myself to the radiation. I read that so many feet away were safe; however, during the night at the hotel I was not feeling well. My husband asked me to go home the next day and stop exposing myself to this strong radiation, reluctantly I agreed.

It all happened so fast my mind was spinning. I was in denial, but I knew deep in my heart I was scared for his life. "God," I asked, "Is this the end of a dream? When I stood in faith for you to send me a husband 21 years ago, I did not mean a short marriage. I meant white hairs, walks on the beach hand in hand, grandchildren chirping in our laps, our daughter's wedding and graduation—sharing it all with my spouse." He has talents that are different from mine and this is why we are attracted to each other. He is a great mathematician, excellent accountant, brilliant businessman and my computer whiz. Exact science is his forte! I am an artist, I create, and my passion is to bring things to life by inventing, planting or designing. I am an aspiring homemaker. I love gardening, sewing, turning a house into a home, constantly rejuvenating the interior and adding to the comfort of our house. I am creative money wise because I am handy. I can paint, build, and originate many things. I experience endless joy and satisfaction while performing these tasks. God gives me an unsurpassed delight witnessing the fruits of my labor. It makes me feel great knowing God made it all possible; it is for glorifying Him in the midst of it, creating it for His honor and adding peace to our home.

All this can become useless in the face of losing a partner. In a second, life can turn upside down, and once meaningful things can lose their fragrance. Out of a colorful life, everything can become black and white. Between the four walls of my hotel room, I was freezing that night and praying that the sunlight would soften my intensified feelings of emptiness and hopelessness. Feeling lonely and unwilling to taste a lifetime of it was what I prayed the most. I wanted to be confident that my husband would come out of it healed. I knew I needed him and I didn't want to be selfish, I trusted he needed me too. I also realized that marriage is much more important in latter season when our mirror image no longer speaks "20," when the color of our hair covets respect, and wisdom accumulated through the years infuses our lives with meaning and purpose. He is my partner, the half that completes me; the shoulder that sustains me, the one God graced me with when I craved family stability. Fragile I was, but even more our daughter needed a dad. He would walk her down the aisle; he would console her if her heart is broken; he would model what a true gentleman ought to be. That I can help with, but not substitute for, I was yearning for assurance that my husband was not losing hope in tomorrow. His presence was imperative and longed for, I was silently praying for his strength and stamina. Beholden for all the people standing in the gap for his health, I was humbled by the overwhelming response. God was faithful as always, and today, although my husband's eye is not completely functional, we all believe that the cancerous tumor is gone. Faith prompts me to declare a victorious healing and a complete recovery.

2016 was my trampoline to 2017. God had a plan and he carried it diligently. He knew my threshold and never tested me beyond my abilities. Faith is the rope between heaven and earth, between Jesus and His beloved ones; but faith can be compromised when hurricanes blast us mercilessly. God has a safety net, and He sends it to us at the moment of free fall without a parachute. In the face of prospective death, when all is black and screaming and so overwhelming, He takes us in His arms and carries us. This is why there is only one set of footprints in the sand.

My Lord, I am kneeling in humble gratefulness; speechless but loved, tired but blessed because without You there would never be me and all of us who desperately need you every second of our lives! When the tears are wiped, and the time to meet you face-to-face comes, we will be ready because You infused us with Your blood and imbued us with Your character, so we can be worthy of Your sacrifice! A profound "Thank you!"—one that goes beyond the hills of the mountains you helped us conquer.

Now I know the meaning of my favorite verse: "I can do all things through Christ who strengthens me"(Philippians 4:13, NKJV)!

2

Beauty for Ashes

To bestow on them a crown of beauty instead of ashes, the oil of joy instead of mourning, and a garment of praise instead of a spirit of despair.
—*Isaiah 61:3, NIV*

As I was calming down, assured that this trial was coming to an end, 2018 started so promising. We decided to take my parents for a mini-vacation in the mountains. We rented a cabin taking our dog Angel with us. The cabin was nestled deep in the forest, embraced by fresh spring colored leaves. The air was buzzing with new awakening; insects and birds were welcoming the warmth of the season invigorated for yet another rebirth. Our beautiful lodging was perched on a hill with the most breathtaking views. As far as the eye can see, on top of the trees, the sunset was gilding the forest with its pallet of golden colors; the rays softly reaching my face were caressing my tired soul. Amazing, peaceful, and relaxing, this atmosphere was exactly what I longed for. We were having our meals on the terrace overlooking a gorgeous panorama. Inhaling tranquility, I was exhaling stress! Thankful and restful, I enjoyed drinking the serenity in realization of my total dependence on God.

Coming back from the forest of the Smoky Mountains was a long and eventful ride. I was thankful to be going home after this change of pace. The summer months were approaching, and I started noticing that our daughter was feeling tired, looking irritated, and visibly losing muscle mass. I made an appointment with her pediatrician, asking him to run a thyroid profile. I saw symptoms that led me to believe she had a problem with her thyroid gland. The doctor requested a test repeat in a month. The results confirmed a hyper function of the gland. On his recommendation we saw a specialist, and she ordered an ultrasound to get a clear picture of the thyroid gland function. The picture revealed abnormal tissue. We were sent immediately to another endocrinologist who performed a biopsy, and what I already dreaded was confirmed: she had cancer.

All three of us were in the room carefully studying the big screen as the needle was protruding the neck tissue. As the unpleasant news was revealed, my jaw dropped; my husband was stunned. We were in shock. Somewhere deep inside me I was hoping and praying that the first cancer indication was a mistake. I was wrong. My heart beat stopped. I turned my eyes up and silently cried out to God, "She is just a young girl. She is not supposed to have cancer . . . Who has such dreadful disease at this age?"

The surgery was scheduled in a week. There were special genetic tests that were sent for confirmation. Once they arrived my baby was ready for surgery. In the early hours of the morning, she was the first one to get to the operating room. I employed many of my friends to pray, standing in the gap for the duration of the surgery. The clock was ticking, and the minutes were passing painfully slow. I was numb and still trying to pray despite myself. I knew my husband was praying too. The surgeon appeared at one point, and a worried expression was written on his face. "Oh n-o-o-o!" I said to myself. "No bad news. Please, Lord. N-o-o-o!" I was not ready to handle anymore negativity. There were complications. The vocal cord was embedded in the gland, and when the gland was taken out, the functionality of the vocal cord dropped to sixty percent. It had been injured while the thyroid gland was extracted. Although the surgeon placed special monitors to follow the outcome, it happened; and he advised us that if the condition of the cord was not improving, he would not be able to proceed. Dr. Fisher needed to place a camera through the nose to assess the throat condition, a very unpleasant procedure. He woke up Vicky, but she did not cooperate; she was turning her head away. In approximately twenty minutes, we heard the news about a second surgery. I was not sure if I was relieved or unhappy. I wished it was all over. At the same time, I trusted the doctor's decision to give the vocal cord time to recuperate.

Three intense months passed. Vicky was worried and dreading the idea of a second surgery. I was not pleased as well, almost wishing the day would never come. It was dark outside in the early morning hours, and very lonely on the road. We headed to the same hospital one more time, hoping for the best and fearing the worst—hoping that once this surgery was over there would be no more hospital visits, and our daughter would be on her way to a complete recovery. Meanwhile, in the back of my mind, I feared that another cancer might be found; and the other vocal cord could be affected, not to mention that one of her parathyroid glands on the right had been removed during the initial extraction. My hope was that the left two glands would remain intact. Knowing parathyroid glands are extremely important for Calcium absorption in the body, I wanted to believe that this time the surgery would be a success, and all organs surrounding the thyroid would remain unharmed.

The second surgery was shorter—instead of three hours, it was two and a half. The doctor assured us that all went as planned. We were relieved and expected Victoria to be fine. She emerged from surgery and arrived in the recovery room, very sleepy and the pain (on a scale of 1-10) was 10. Her cry was painful to watch. The nurse gave her an intravenous pain reliever. It took a long time to kick in, but the pain never really subsided. After the first surgery, the recovery process was much shorter. We assumed it would be the same. To our surprise, we stayed for hours; the pain was strong and persistent. Late that afternoon we headed home. All of us were exhausted and sleep deprived. Victoria was moaning the entire time, absolutely drained from the experience. My husband and I were mentally and physically worn out. There was nothing else we could do. Watching our child suffer was debilitating and awfully agonizing.

It was not over. Victoria was in a lot of discomfort for the following weeks. I kept giving her pain medications and made her sleep any minute of the day. Her pain continued during the Christmas holidays. By the end of the year, she was still in constant pain. I was not able to react— my tank was empty; my body was beyond the point of exhaustion. I was acting robotically, trying to give attention and love as much as I could squeeze from my emptiness. It was God's grace that sustained me. His love was surrounding His precious girl, my sweet child. She was first His before she became mine. With this knowledge, I was putting one foot before the other, grateful that Jesus was my partner. My husband was so comforting. Deep down he was hurting, but his strength was a blessing. We were all in a quiet realization that this suffering made the bond between us stronger than ever. My husband, the sole financial supporter, was brave, paying hospital bills and acting calmly around Victoria. His job is extremely demanding, being a CPA working as a reconciliation head manager for a prominent financial company. The stress level is off the charts. He needed a presence of mind to concentrate on work. Vicky needed us more than ever, as we needed her to be healthy and happy again.

2019 came with three ER visits. The first unexpected visit was due to excruciating pain in the surgical area, stomach, and Vicky's ear. We ended up there at midnight and came home in the early hours of the day. My husband had a few hours to recharge and went to work the morning after. I was sure he was at the end of his strength, but he was a hero—he never said a word about it. My spouse is one of those people who hardly ever complain about pain or tiredness; he just squeezes his teeth and keeps on going. I slept and woke up looking forward to a day of picking up the pieces where I had left off. So many things get neglected when health becomes an issue. It was vital for us to be healthy in order to care for each other. I was secretly hoping to catch up on more rest for both Victoria and me. The reality was different.

All plans were suddenly interrupted by another family member's eminent need; it was our canine baby. Moaning in agony, I have never seen Angel in so much affliction and anguish! In the afternoon we went to the vet where we found out he had a pinched nerve. Poor pooch was not allowed to jump, go up the stairs, or climb the furniture. He was prescribed steroids and pain killers, and the first evening after he hurt his back he ate nothing. Oh, my heart went out to him! To top it all off, several days into the treatment, the dog started having blood in the stool. We were advised to stop all medication, but the bleeding became substantial. Angel was admitted to the vet hospital for two days and one night. Intravenous hydration, several injections, and no food were the medical instructions. He looked sad and in obvious discomfort.

All was coming on big waves. Was there an end to it, or was I having an awful nightmare which would finish the minute I opened my eyes? Oh, how much I wished I had a dream, but it was so real and so difficult to absorb. I sat on the couch that evening, trying to remember the last time I laughed and saw my family well.

My birthday arrived, and, for the first time in a long while, I saw light; I saw hope; I saw peace that day. I was happy and so inspired. I believed deep down that the New Year came with a new agenda, that God brought an answer to my heartfelt prayers and was seeing us through the storm. The sky was clear; the rain stopped; and clouds were blown away. I received beautiful cream colored, long-stemmed roses from my husband, and my daughter brought breakfast in bed for me. Plus, there was a lovely card from Vicky, Bill, and Angel, specially designed for my birthday. My dear friend Hannah, whom I hadn't seen for quite some time, came to visit; and, together with my husband and daughter, we all had a few amazing hours over coffee. People kept sending sweet wishes, even after the date. Everyone's gesture was warming my heart. I was elated. I felt loved. That day I glimpsed into the future and experienced what my heart had longed for quite some time. Like a candle in the night, the flame slowly faded, and only the smoke from the fragrant wick reminded me of the meaningful day and what could have been, if only diseases did not interrupt . . .

How much I delight in the little gestures and the big ones. How amazing a few words can be when the soul is hungry for beauty, instead of ashes, my heart was yearning for change. It also hungered for new experiences that break the redundancies of pain and suffering. "Give me more joy, Lord. Give me my daughter's smile. Let my husband cease being quietly sad." My soul was begging, "I want to see my dog wag his tail without ache and struggle." I kept pouring out my thoughts silently, "I know Your time is not coinciding with mine; You know best when to bring an answer. Just that all seems so long, Lord please, it is absolutely unbearable to wait." I almost cried, "Do I or my family need more tests to endure? Do we all need to be taught a lesson? Or did the devil have an agenda, and his arrows were a desperate attempt to bring our guards down, because he knew Your plan, My Lord, a plan that includes securing our lives and our well-being? Your plans are always big and well designed and, most importantly, never fail. Who can compare to the King of the Universe?"

Silence . . . but silence is not necessarily bad; it most likely is an agreement that the end is near.

I could almost hear my God speaking softly, "I am here right beside you, and I heard you… do not be afraid I am in control."

"You do not need to speak to give peace, Father; your peace surpasses all human understanding. What is next?" I whispered in a desperate attempt to hear more about positive change. I prayed fervently, anticipating that I would see change sooner rather than later. I had a conviction that, despite the obvious results, healing was coming our way. Now, my mind had no capacity to think anymore. God is a God of promises, and His promises can never be in vain. I trust the biblical promises: "I will restore health to you, and your wounds I will heal" says the Lord in (Jeremiah 30:17, ESV).

All I ever wanted was to have my family healthy. This was an absolute must. Without it, many other things become meaningless, and fun completely dulls until it disappears from our view. Pain is something I wish to no one. I walked slowly outside and in the garden I turned my head towards the sky, and, when I saw the stars, I was reminded that I have strong faith in Jesus. This faith that encompasses hope has brought so much positive emotions through the years in parts for my husband's life and many other circumstances. Almost impossible situations amazingly turned out to be the best experiences ever. Witnessing plenty of answered prayers had given me endurance. Even when I don't see immediate results, I have the stamina to wait, knowing deep down that something is about to change. I know for certain Who has the capacity to do this, and I exhale with relief.

Jesus tells us that if we believe without a doubt in our hearts, what we believe will come to pass; therefore, a positive attitude is better than a sorrowful soul. "A cheerful heart is good medicine, but a crushed spirit dries up the bones" (Proverbs 17:22, NIV). There was a time for tears, and now I needed time for laughter and a time for rejoicing (cf: Ecclesiastes 3). I had to wash my face, comb my hair, and call peace upon my attitude. After all, my downcast soul needed to exult. I am who I am because God lifts me up and holds me dear.

"The end," I declared, "is today! . . . And I will not allow the evil to triumph!" Victoriousness is a trademark reserved only for my Savior. My Jehovah-Rapha (Hebrew for God who heals) triumphs over all and exaltation belongs to His people. "I have witnessed miracles of healing in my own life; therefore, God is healing every member of my family. " I declared. This knowledge somehow overtook me like it was coming straight from above. God's healing is always complete. Answered prayers and visions confirm the veracity of such healings all the time. This is the ultimate reward for those who rely on Jesus Christ. I am one of them.

My days are now engulfed in recovery and cure, and my anticipation for the future is to keep it that way. My dog is healthy today—no more pain on his back or blood from his stomach. I prayed for him too. After all, he is one of God's precious creations and my canine child. My daughter does not bear cancer anymore: it all went on the cross, and she is restored in the wounds of our Savior. My husband no longer has the malignant tumor in his eye. I am grateful that God is in control and health belongs to my home. I believe, and my faith is based on past experiences and future expectations, but, mainly, all is rooted deeply in the Word.

Amen to all, and ". . . as for me and my house, we will serve the LORD" (Joshua 24:15, KJB).

We ". . . will not die, but live, and . . . will proclaim what the Lord has done" (Psalm 118:17, NET).

How assured I am that all has completely ceased. I can sing and dance again in the presence of my Creator. I shall give Him all the glory; I am giving Him all the glory now, knowing He is right beside me. Suffering or not, He is there, and His palm has mine in it. I was walking in the shadow of the valley of death, but He is guiding me. His staff and His nearness, they are comforting me (cf: Psalm 23). I hear His voice calling me on the other side of the dark tunnel, where light shines brightly. Those moments are the most difficult while in the darkness, to keep the faith in the midst of the storm. Our earthly life is infused with trials, and stumbling, and falling, and bleeding; but, when our blood becomes blended with the blood of Jesus, a miracle happens. Then, we get supernatural strength, power, and stoicism. For, only then, can we withstand the raging winds and merciless waters. Only then, our tears become diamonds that sparkle in the sun of healing. The day Jesus was on the cross our chains were broken; His grace became our trophy, and we were claimed as children of a Mighty King. What can a man do to me when I have the Ruler of the Universe on my side? Only through Jesus I am strong—I do not recognize myself. The Lord has changed me as though I am a new creation and has adorned me with His character and His stability. He clothed me with new feelings; a new mantle is upon my shoulders. The heavens had proclaimed the glory of God; I can shout the name Emmanuel (God with us) joyfully!

Today is a new day, and, with humility, I realize that without my friend Jesus I would have been unable to meet the dawn. I am endlessly grateful that I am not a disbeliever, rejecting our biblical Father. My days are numbered, but the day I meet my Daddy in heaven I will get to spend joyous moments in His presence.

What is a human life in the face of the hereafter? Just like a delicate white fluff carried by the wind of uncertainty for miles and miles, at the end lost in the branches of a tree or wetted in the cold riverbanks of life's hypocrisy, ever to be forgotten. Our lives melt like a snowflake on a warm winter morning, and the memory of our existence grows faint the moment we pass from this life into the infinite.

Fear turns into boldness, just knowing that the best is yet to come. Many earthly gains become meaningless in the face of heaven's reality where we will spend forever on golden streets, within precious stone gardens, among angelic creatures, and all but happiness will fill our days.

No more hurt, no more tears, no more death and loss. Our heavenly Father grants beauty for ashes, boldness for fear, joy for mourning, peace and calmness for despair (cf: Isaiah 61:3).

Love—the ultimate prize and the most undeserved, but given to us by grace—that, my friend, is what we call a God who laid down his life for you and me! Today, I experience the testimony in (John 3:16) and perceive how real and true it is! His promises are eternal, and His words everlasting.

In the end, because of His unfailing loving care, we should strive to make our Lord proud, so we can gleam in His splendor. His light should shine through us, so God can touch the lost souls, the very ones He gave His utmost Love for!!!

This is my song for you, Papa. I will keep singing . . .

> "For God loved the world so much that he gave his one and only Son, so that everyone who believes in him will not perish but have eternal life. God sent his Son into the world not to judge the world, but to save the world through him" (John 3:16-17, NLT).

3

Walking on a Tiny Thread Between Life and Death

So do not fear, for I am with you; do not be dismayed,
for I am your God. I will strengthen you and help you;
I will uphold you with my righteous right hand.
—Isaiah 41:10, NIV

God took a ball of clay and created a masterpiece, making me one of a kind. He does it with all of His children. No matter how the world views me, I know my heavenly father's opinion matters most. This notion is hard to accept in the face of public criticism; there is widespread desire to conform us to the world's standards. People want to put us in a box limiting our potential, willing to discount us because they have certain examples in their minds of who we need to be. But God has different plans for us. His reality is limitless. His ideas go to the ends of the universe, so He frees us to become who we are designed to be -- deeply intellectual and brilliantly inspired beings. There are no boundaries with Jesus; there are only possibilities. We are granted talents that are born out of the depths of our souls, inspired by the Holy Spirit. Our image is fashioned after God's grandiose one. We are created in the likeness of a majestic Creator, the ruler of the universe whose strokes are unsurpassed.

Are you not yet wowed? I am! And still today I hold dear the verses in Psalm 139:

> For you formed my inward parts; you covered me in my mother's womb. I will praise you for I am fearfully and wonderfully made; marvelous are your works, and that my soul knows very well. My frame was not hidden from you, when I was made in secret, and skillfully wrought in the lowest parts of the earth. Your eyes saw my substance, being yet unformed. (Psalm 139:13-16a, NKJV)

God planned our lives "before the foundation of the world, to be holy and blameless in love before him" (Ephesians 1:4, CSB). In light of this verse, my life was permeated with astonishing experiences. They were at both spectrums of the extreme—very human and very spiritual. For the first part of my existence in Europe, God planned encounters with one objective in mind: to reveal His power to save lives. The second part on the North American continent was pervaded with supernatural experiences. Almighty Lord designed my life so carefully and intentionally. From Adam and Eve until today we were, are, and will all be on the drafting board—mindfully created with the utmost care. With each individual God intends a story that is flabbergasting, all because He loves us endlessly and desires us to spend eternity in His company. I never stop being captivated by His choices; I like them. I try to understand the meaning behind them. He is establishing His sovereignty plus purposefully teaching us to rely on Him more and more—helping us become stronger in our weakness, shedding light on the truth that we are capable through Him to do anything.

Ever so fascinated by God's methods and revelations, I discovered the answer to a lifelong question in the pages of the Bible. The question was, "Why did God spare my life three times?"

My parents were both working very hard—my mom told me that in order to have a decent living, both of them had to be employed. Yes, this was the beginning of my parents' marriage. Later, their life improved tremendously. In order to work and care for me, they placed me in a weekly childcare. I was born in a home where my dad's sisters and family shared a house with us. It was the house my father and his two sisters were born and grew up in. After we separated into two different homes, our households were divided as well. I was two years old at the time, and I needed a babysitter. I was surrounded with love and attention prior to the separation, and my world must have crumbled to pieces when I was left among many needy children with one care giver who knew nothing about me. With no emotional attachments, we were all routinely cared for. Unknown to my parents, I was neglected and left to cry for days. My mom had called to inquire about me, but she was assured that I was perfectly o.k. The first weekend she came to take me home, only to discover that I was in a state of total dehydration. In her words, I looked like a vegetable deprived of water. The doctor later informed her that I was at the verge of death if left only a few more hours. Later, she learned that the staff left me without water or food because I was crying uncontrollably. God intervened, and moments before my death, He sent my mother to the rescue; I had my first gift of life. To my knowledge, I never went back to the childcare.

A few years passed by, and I was four already when I learned about another story. The truth is it was so dramatic that, to this day, I still remember details of what happened next. My mom was coloring her hair, and I recall how thirsty I had become. Since I could not yet reach the sink, I asked my mom to give me a glass of water. I asked once. I asked twice. And on the third attempt, she still did not give me water. Later she told me she had asked me to be patient until she finished a task, but I was thirsty and I was not giving up. Out of the corner of my eye, I saw a glass filled with a transparent liquid. That signaled water in my mind, so I headed in the direction of the glass, happy that I found an answer to my problem.

This glass was within reach—it was situated on top of the shoe bench. I reached for the tiny glass, and, with such immense satisfaction, I poured the unknown liquid into my mouth and down my throat. Only milliseconds passed when I started gasping for air. There, in this tiny glass, my mom had poured fully concentrated color developer!

This chemical was burning my insides like crazy. I was going to die if my mom did not act in a split second. The moment she realized what I had devoured, she forcefully poured milk into my throat and made me vomit, continuing with water. I was so tired from not being able to breathe. I was choking, vomiting, and crying. I was in a state of shock, but my mom courageously passed the test. After this ordeal she took me to the hospital where a thorough examination determined that I was o.k. The doctor told my mom that she did the only thing that saved my life—water to neutralize the strong acid, which could have destroyed my esophagus and ultimately killed me. I ingested a very strong poison. She also made me vomit, so this poison did not reach my stomach. It could have been extremely damaging there as well. Water also dilutes and lessens the effect of bases or acids because water has a pH of seven, meaning neutral. This is why, when hair is being colored, it is initially rinsed with water to stop the processing.

Until today, I am grateful to my mom who had earned only *A*'s in chemistry, her favorite subject. This is the truth: she kept her presence of mind and acted boldly because, if she had panicked, there would have been irreversible damage and ultimate death. God did it again: He saved me for the second time.

I was very young and the attacks on my life looked so sudden and purposeful. The truth is I was too young to comprehend the difference between life and death. The intrusion on my life was a complete puzzle, yet today I am convinced the evil one wanted my delicate existence to come to a complete halt.

Years passed and I became a teenager. One amazing summer I was visiting the Sea Riviera. Every year my aunt and I enjoyed a two-week vacation. I loved these fantastic, fun filled days—sun, sand, and freedom. Life in the capital was associated with the mountains being just minutes away by public transportation. Weekends were fun in the mountains. This is what many city residents were doing—enjoying the fresh air and quiet atmosphere of the serene mountains during a weekend holiday. Temperate climates have beautiful vegetation, soft green grass, and excellent weather; not to mention the very low humidity found in my first country, approximately thirty percent throughout the year.

So, going on vacation at the sea was a treat for schoolchildren like me. We looked forward to summer vacation; and, interestingly enough, those at the mountains dreamed of seagulls, bare feet, and sand between the toes. Those at the sea dreamed of cool air, brisk walks, and the fresh smell of pinecones.

At thirteen, I still did not know how to swim, so my aunt seized the task of teaching me. The day was warm, and, in the morning after breakfast, the routine was to head out to the seashore. The sea was not calm: it had waves and strong undercurrent, and we decided to stay very close to the shoreline. I just made two steps and literally lost the bottom. My hand slipped off my aunt's hand and I was lost. All I remember was water surrounding me, strange sensation when there is no sky above you or bottom beneath you. I lost the sense of up and down. My thoughts were only, "Is this the end?" This time I knew that I might be dying, and I was scared and confused. I do not know how long I was under water. In such extreme situations we lose the notion of time. While I was still debating if I were leaving this earth, I felt two hands under my arms, and seconds later I was placed on the sand and questioned if I was o.k. I did not know the answer to this question. I was still absolutely delirious. Later, I learned that I had been sucked down by a whirlpool steps from the shore, but my aunt, being a good swimmer, managed to come to the surface and started screaming for help. The lifeguards heard her and rescued me. From this day on, I knew that the experience would put a permanent mark on my relationship with water. I never really learned how to dive nor completely mastered the skill of swimming. Often, fear creeps in and warns me to be cautious around deep water, everywhere. Despite all this, I love the ocean; I love the music of the splashing waves. There is something so romantic in a stroll along the seashore. The footprints in the sand are a sweet reminder of a moment that forever flies, and if we do not grab it, we are missing out on incredible increments of a colorful quilt called life. Breathing deep iodine fumes at the stony shore is actually very healthy and always brings back childhood memories. The smell of salty water transfers me back to very happy times in another life. My aunt died ten years ago, but I am still indebted to her for saving my life, and to the lifeguard whose name I never learned so I could thank him.

Yes, I feel as though I lived two separate lives—one that was back in Europe and one here in the States.

Three times I came back from seemingly tragic situations; three times my life was hanging between here and eternity; and three times the Almighty stepped in, sending angels to hover over me. I could feel God's selfless love very distinctly. Is it because God was planning to accomplish something through me that was bigger than life? Is it because when He created me, He had a master plan where I played a crucial role; and all attempts on my life were truly great examples of how only God can save us? Maybe both, and I know for certain that He first loved me more than I could ever know. It is so comforting knowing we are created as children of an incredible Father. Every soul on earth is a showpiece of the greatest sculptor ever known, whose astounding love and grace keeps us alive and well. I know this full well. Since then, He has used me in various situations for purposes that are so dear to me, but mainly for His glory. I love my calling as a Bible school teacher. I also love talking to people about Jesus, so these examples singlehandedly are enough in His eyes. He does not have unrealistic expectations of perfect performances. He knows we are imperfect, He also knows what we are capable of; therefore, whatever we do He is happy we are trying our best to serve Him.

Life is a delicate notion. It can be interrupted instantly, so I sincerely hope everyone reading today knows for certain where they are headed, because, once the journey starts and we take our last breath of air on earth, there is no coming back. Trust me, I visited heaven and the only way there-is up. If you are headed in the opposite direction, the eternity that will be revealed is an absolute nightmare. Choose Jesus today, and become His follower, because tomorrow is never promised, and it may be too late. I wish you a great future. Remember God loves all creation immeasurably, and He has great hopes for everyone. Shalom!

4

The Day I Learned About Jesus

You will seek me and find me when you seek me with all your heart.
—Jeremiah 29:13, NIV

Silver necklace given to me as a present, it reads: -Gott Schutze Dich-meaning in German-God Bless You.

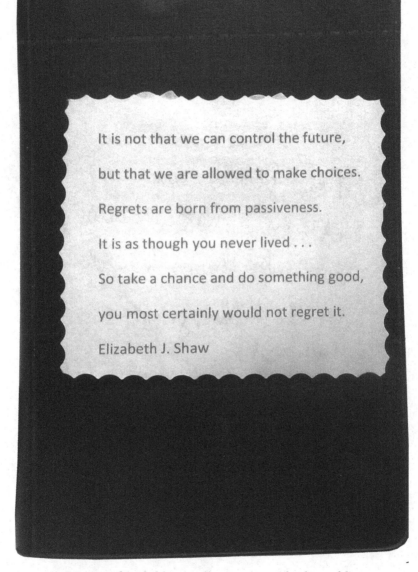

It is not that we can control the future,

but that we are allowed to make choices.

Regrets are born from passiveness.

It is as though you never lived . . .

So take a chance and do something good,

you most certainly would not regret it.

Elizabeth J. Shaw

My very first bible, small in print with plastic blue covers; it still remains my prized treasure.

This is what Edelhand, a kind, Austrian, Christian lady wrote on the pages of the first bible I received from her in Vienna, Austria.

The day I became intrigued by God changed my life forever. This day was like no other I remember it so distinctly. It was back in a land east of the Atlantic Ocean. I was walking on a sidewalk in the springtime. The sun was warming the ground; fragrant fresh air was waking up the world. I lifted my head towards the sky, asking "Who is God?"

I was a curious teenager. My aunt had given me a cross necklace. I had another present as well a little necklace that read: "Gott Schutze Dich," meaning "God Bless You." I wore both close to my heart and only recently decided to translate the meaning of the German inscription. How amazing! I was blessed before I knew what the writing on the back meant!

Christianity was established in the year 865 by a ruler named Boris back in times that were quite intricate. So, the Christian church was a place to find peace and oneness with God—a place where people were coming to light candles, surrounded by icons and scenes of the Old and New Testament meticulously depicted on walls and windows, ceilings and doors. I guess many were searching for a power higher than us then. During the days of my existence people continued searching for closeness with their Creator. Some of the church attendants personally knew God, and some only mechanically repeated certain rituals but, like me, never really asked, "Who is the Almighty?" I was not comfortable to ask anyone. Priests were to be respected but not conversed with. I did not know how to approach them. Maybe it was lack of knowledge, maybe fear. To be on the safe side, I chose to remain silent. Bible? To my knowledge there were no Bibles. Christian literature was not sold in stores.

We celebrated Christmas and Easter. My Aunt Mimi would recite the Lord's Prayer. She used to have Biblical studies as a little girl. My younger aunt, Kate, was Christian as well. My father had Biblical studies in school as a young boy too. All of this was so long in the past. Times had changed; we were never introduced to Jesus at school. Those things were hush-hush, discussed only at home behind closed doors. Students were not allowed to wear crosses or talk about Christian topics of any kind. It all seemed rather elusive and mystical. The reason? Communism.

I distinctly remember one of my attempts to pray in church. It was the neighborhood church called Holy Trinity. I went there before an exam. I had no idea how to proceed or what to say. I simply muttered something like, "Please God help me pass this test," lighted a candle, made a sign of the cross, and left the church. I did not get an 'A' as I was hoping. So, my first prayer was a fruitless attempt, and I lost faith in prayers. It was silly to be defined by one failed attempt. Little did I know, this was the devil's purposeful agenda to prevent me from trusting Christ. When there are no Bibles, one needs a personal revelation from heaven, like Paul who was stopped in his tracks. God wants us to read the Gospel where we will learn the truth and be freed from ignorance. "Then you will know the truth, and the truth will set you free" (John 8:32, NIV).

I clearly had no knowledge of the truth about Jesus; my prayers had no substance, but I had needs. However, I was like a kid in a store: "Please God give me free candy." This is not how it should work. God does not grant selfish wishes or succumb to demands. He grants heartfelt, meaningful, sincere prayers; prayers that come from the depths of our hearts and speak the truth in love. "I love them that love me, and those that seek me . . . shall find me" (Proverbs 8:17, KJV).

Oh, Lord. I was seeking You. I was searching my own heart and the sky for You . . .

After graduating high school, I was accepted into a musical school. This was the time I became anxious to finally read the Bible. I started asking who might own one; and I learned that my father's aunt had one. Fear crept anew . . . *If I ask for a Bible, I might do something spiritually forbidden.* I was having doubts. *Was I doing something wrong? Is God untouchable, strict, even merciless?* He actually loved me, but I was unaware. Again, my courage was not enough to ask my relative, and all just faded away. Now, I see the mark of the beast keeping me—through fear—far from my Lord.

I was 19 when I received my first Bible, but so far away from home in a foreign land where we were political emigrants. A kind, Austrian,

Christian lady handed me my very first Bible. Small in print with soft blue covers, this Bible is still my precious possession to this very day. I will never forget this woman. With so much love, she wrote wishes for me on the front cover: "Viel Glück im 'freien' Westen und dass alle ihre Wünsche in Erfüllung gehen, . . .Edelhand und Bobi V. 27.6.86." It's German for "Good luck in the 'free' West and may all your wishes be fulfilled, . . .Edelhand and Bobi V. June 27, 1986." Bobi was her husband. She would forever be embedded in my memory. Her gesture became extremely meaningful as time passed. She may never learn what an essential tool she turned out to be in my spiritual growth. "Those who know your name trust in you, for you, Lord, have never forsaken those who seek you" (Psalm 9:10, NIV). Thankfully this verse became a reality.

The day I gave my life to Jesus was another extraordinary experience. God picked my dearest friend Sarah, who was a spiritual mom but now is a confidant with whom I share prayers and stand in the gap for people, for America, for urgent family needs. God uses us beautifully, not only to have lifting conversations and learn from each other, but to pray and have visions for people, places, and needs of various kinds. A prophet said that we were like "the bread and the soup"—in other words, complementing each other in a spiritual sense. The Lord chose this union to stand because He is pleased in it. The human factor of this relationship is not as important as the spiritual one. She advised me to read the Bible, so I can find the truthful answers for myself from the One True Source. She has never given me an advice to do wrong by anyone. Always positive, always encouraging, always asking me to be responsible for my actions, she encourages me to pray for my enemies and forgive them just like the Bible is teaching us. We both serve an Awesome God.

I recall how we met for the first time. So sudden and genuine was our first moment of "Hello my name is . . ." I had seen her once prior to this meeting and, anxious to tell me, she boldly started. My parents and I used to live a block from the ocean; there we both sat at the kitchen table. She made small talk for a minute, and then she looked me straight in the eye and asked if I knew Jesus. This was a moment of truth and dare; I had wanted to know Him for quite some time, so

25

that was my chance to do so. My heart flickered; I felt a boost of energy that flamed inside me for the first time. Sarah told me as much as she felt necessary about the Lord, but all I remember was whether I wanted Jesus as my Savior, and if I was ready to accept Him in my life. I did ask for forgiveness of my sins, and that marked the beginning of my amazing relationship with my amazing Father.

Sarah is the one person I know who would pick up the phone in the middle of the night if I called. She has never refused a prayer, nor she turned away any of my heartfelt requests. Such people are a rare find; they come once in a lifetime. They are gifts from above. You open them and they shine like a star in a dark night. Sparks fly from them, and they represent your innermost desire for something so fantastically special like God Himself. They are the Biblical Jonathans from 1 Samuel, the best friend David had, who despite his father's hatred for David, was faithful till the end. We all need a Jonathan in our lives, but even more blessed are those who have him or her as a best friend. God must love me a lot because He gave me Sarah!

I believe this is one of the reasons God opened a wide door for us to come here. America became my sweet home away from home. Here I met Jesus the strongest love of my life; I met Sarah; I met my sisters-in-Christ. Here, I prayed for two years, and God sent my wonderful husband. Here my daughter was born and became the center of our love, the connection that completed us. Here God sent blessings that enriched and established our family. Here, I believe, God will continue to grow my faith, and here He will enlarge His territory. Here among the flowers and colorful birds on the banks of a picturesque lake, full of ducks, fish, and turtles, is my home. The sunsets are amazing! The view is breathtaking. The location is perfect, and the grass is so green; it feels good to look at it but even more so to lie on it and count endless fluffy clouds. I have a garden, and the swing is my favorite spot in the afternoon when the white airy balls in the sky turn purple, pink, and baby blue as the sun peacefully but spectacularly beautiful sets in the west. The night jasmine spreads its aroma, and the crickets turn on the music that lulls me into dreams.

Sunsets, are the culmination point of the day, they come with such grandiose explosion of colors and beauty, God sends, "Sweet dreams to the world, and gently pulls the covers so we can have a restful night." I am blessed to witness them every evening one more amazing than the other. . .

On the banks of this gorgeous lake we have been witnessing gracious swans and Muscovy, Mallard, White, Dabbling, Domestic, Blue Winged Teal, and Moorhens ducks, turtles and fish; colorful birds nesting among the flowery bushes. Each morning we are romanced by the inspirational chirping and unique vocalization of birds that wake us up softly.

I have spent most of my adult life in this land, and I can say in full confidence, "I love this country!" My oldest friend Deborah is from my days in college. We share so many memories. She is someone I can pick up with from where we left off and feel like we just saw each other yesterday. With her we share our carefree youth and adulthood memories and they are endless but precious. I've lived in the same town for 17 years. Some of my neighbors are a vital part of my journey. I can name one in particular—Hannah who plays an important role in the life of this book. We used to have long nightly talks about the Lord, and I remember how much I looked forward to those talks. After a long day, I needed the energizing boost of Jesus, and Hannah was like a medicine for my soul.

My life is bubbling. There are moments I am sad and desperate for answers. There are others, when I am elated and on top of the world, but, at the end of the day, I am thankful that I am part of this nation. Here, freedom is still in existence, and my faith is not jeopardized. I am not prosecuted for being a Christian, and God holds a central part in my reality.

Tiqevott Gedolott--in Hebrew meaning Great Hopes. Prophetic heavens are open, and God sends incredible signs that invigorate my entire life. A rich Christian inheritance is being bestowed upon me. New revelations are reaching me in every direction. I am honored to be a part of the big picture where God is Lord, and He is on His throne ruling, crowned in splendor, granting me blessings every single day. I know where I am today. Tomorrow is yet to come, but, when it does, I will surely be wiser and more acquainted with my Creator. One day He will mount a white horse and come to sweep me off my feet. But, until then, I will wait patiently. Now "I will . . . lay me down in peace, and sleep: for thou, LORD, only makest me dwell in safety" (Psalm 4:8, KJB).

This is a picture of my father inside his masterpiece. This copper sculpture of a woman still exists and last time we saw it my dad posed for a picture next to it.

My father with his Mom and Dad walking in the capital downtown what a beautiful family. My amazing grandmamma and grandpapa I miss knowing them especially granddad I never really met him. He was killed long before I was born.

This pin was given to me by a flight attendant from TWA (Trans World Airlines). The airlines that we boarded in Vienna, Austria and arrived with in New York City on September 17, 1986.

5

Wake Up America...
The Meaning of Freedom

So do not fear, for I am with you; do not be dismayed,
for I am your God. I will strengthen you and help you;
I will uphold you with my righteous right hand.
—Isaiah 41:10, NIV

The Lord is my strength and my song; he has given me victory.
—Exodus 15:2, NLT

My dad is a sculptor; this is his true calling. At the time I was twelve, thirteen years old, he discovered his talent. He had a degree in architecture and construction, but God had other plans for his future. He won a competition in creative sculpting and became one of the well-known sculptors in the country.

Although his specialty was copper, he was incorporating wood, terracotta, ceramic, gold, and other precious metals into his showpieces. He created numerous masterpieces. To this day his art is displayed in almost every town back home. We only have pictures to remind us. One of my favorite is my daddy inside a big figure of a woman made out of copper. Later, in Austria where we were granted political asylum, my dad was offered a job at a museum restoring art.

We chose to leave Europe and headed for the United States, because Austria was too close to the communist bloc. We had every reason to fear the tentacles of this regime. My parents' lives and families had been destroyed by the communist establishment.

My paternal grandparents had a beautiful family of five. They owned a house with a big yard. My grandma was a fashion designer; she had a small business at home with several employees. Her business was thriving because she was talented and imaginative. As a business partner and active member on the board of directors for a prominent sewing factory, she was a savvy businesswoman. My grandfather was an agent at the Division of Alcohol and Tobacco Control. They were Christians, attending the local church, and life was peaceful until political regimes changed, and the communists took over.

Times were uncertain; people were devastated; and the cruelty started in full force. Landowners were losing control of their land by political directives, forcing them into cooperatives, losing proprietorship of their own land. Businesses were seized by party agenda, nationalizing everything. Only the political elite had rights and privileges; everyone else was on the watch list. Many people lost their lives and disappeared without a trace. The desire to control an individual's behavior by oppressing the mind, to subdue the masses by destroying their desire for creativity and freedom—this was a well-executed goal.

My grandfather became a victim of this cruel master plan. He belonged to an organization that fought the chauvinist propaganda and was pro-freedom from communism. Incarcerated on numerous occasions, interrogated, and beaten, he was returned home, not knowing when he would be taken back to be tortured again.

His family was terrorized with constant searches at various times, without warning or concern for individual privacy. Everything of value was seized without proper documentation or authority. The house was left bare and broken. The residents were not allowed to visit the restroom during these raids. As a result of these experiences, my dad has a fear of closed spaces; he has to suffer with claustrophobia as part of his life.

One unfortunate day, my grandfather was taken for the last time and placed in a death camp, one of the most heinous camps. Almost no one survived the cruelty experienced there. My aunt recalls that he was not fed; all clothing was confiscated, and he was left with only a t-shirt and torn pants. The barracks where the prisoners slept were in deplorable condition; no bathrooms or accommodations for food preparation existed within the premises. They were provided with little or no food; some were left to starve. People were forced into hard labor, suffering periods of torture and inhumane treatment. Camp laborers were brutalized on a daily basis, beaten with sandbags placed on top of their bodies to mask visible injuries, but inside organs were destroyed. Death was prolonged and agonizing.

The one time my aunt had a chance to visit, she saw her father for just ten minutes, freezing in the cold of winter. She attempted to give him her coat, but the guard slapped her hands and did not allow this to happen. A foul smell surrounded the mass graves of those who were viciously murdered and whose bodies were strewn like garbage. He was a shell of the man my aunt had known, now a man of skin and bones, broken by his captors. My grandfather endured more than five long years of torture and mistreatment. Twenty some months have passed and no news from my grandfather had made his family assume he was dead. Suddenly in 1950 the family received his clothes without explanation of his death or the whereabouts of his remains. The family was convinced he too was executed and discarded into one of those mass graves. To this day we have no knowledge of where his remains are buried. No death certificate was issued; all documentation was purposely burned, leaving no trace of the cruel acts performed in those death camps.

During this period my grandmother was left alone with three children and a need to provide them a means for survival. Her business was shut down and they were forced into poverty. While my grandfather was still alive, she courageously decided to visit the police department and ask for her husband's location. The consequences of this visit were devastating: my grandmother was savagely raped. Her children recall her returning home with blood-stained and torn clothing at 1:00 a.m. after eight agonizing hours. As soon as she removed those garments, she burned them in the fireplace. The invasion of her privacy had traumatic results; she remained silent. There was intense fear in her eyes, and the children knew she had an unimaginable experience. Later, my grandma was diagnosed with schizophrenia. She made numerous attempts to take her own life but was always caught by someone; God wanted her to live.

The care of the family was left in the hands of a fragile teenage girl, my oldest aunt. In her stories she shared how she would use the wooden floor for firewood. She walked to the nearest park to gather extra wood for warming; money was nonexistent. My father's friend would give his own breakfast—one slice of bread with butter and honey—to my father while they were walking to school. Before continuing on to school, Daddy would return home with that slice of bread where it would be divided amongst the three children and my grandma. This meal was the only source of food for many days. As they grew older, my aunt and my dad found odd jobs, allowing them to bring home some nourishment for the family. My younger aunt was keeping house and caring for her sick mom.

One story stands out, and I still vividly recall the details my dad shared. As a teenager, he found work for a full day and returned home with a bill of twenty, enough to buy three loafs of bread; this would have been the meal for almost a week for the entire family. He was showing his sisters the money, when a strong draft from the door blew the bill into the fireplace. They all stood with wide-opened eyes and broken dreams of food that never reached the table. How poor, neglected, and lonely they were not belonging anywhere. Although they had a mom, she did not have the capacity to care for the children, so they were nearly orphans. My daddy was grateful to his older sisters for everything, and later in time he took the initiative to care for his siblings and his mom. He felt a moral obligation and carried it out with love.

He never forgot the torments of his past . . . when he married Mom, he shared his dream of leaving his country when the first opportunity was presented to them. They made several attempts to escape, but these attempts were unsuccessful because the police would not allow us to travel as a family. Dad's plan was to have all three of us leave together.

One summer my dad was assembling his sculptures for a museum in a historical city. There he met the president of the National Automotive Association and both became acquainted. Later, the president was given a very pricey gift from my father, a sculpture dipped in gold. In return for this gift, my family was issued overseas passports which allowed us to travel to Austria for a month vacation. The true reason for our trip was never revealed, because the country was still under communist rule. This would be our escape.

I had a very sought-after opera voice, and, on recommendation of my voice instructor, we planned to visit a well-known vocal specialist and further my education in Vienna. This plan was never executed . . . if only I lived in a different time and place . . . if only I was not born into communism.

The truth about escaping was kept a secret. Not even our closest relatives or friends were aware of our plan; we were protecting our loved ones because we knew they would be interrogated by the authorities. After we left, both my father's and mother's sisters were called by the police department on numerous occasions and told to write down what they knew. No one believed that they had no knowledge of our plan to emigrate.

It was on November 30, 1985, with three tiny suitcases and an immeasurable amount of courage, at three o'clock in the morning, we took the stairs and left our precious home, never to see it again. Our apartment was later confiscated unlawfully by the government; we would never again pass through its doors. The memories remained hidden in the silent walls of the premises. Once, my family lived there leaving behind our mark, laughter, tears, conversations, and cherished aspirations . . . if walls were able to talk . . .

Years passed; the dreams we dreamed and conversations we led in our precious home echoed within our hearts; and only we, together, could share meaningful stories. I have a black and white picture of the building and the balcony where I spent my evenings at dusk dreaming about my family's future. On this balcony I grew cactus plants in small pots, and I was convinced that if one of my plants bloomed, we would succeed in escaping the country. God did it, but in my mind, I was convinced that the sign of the bloom was somehow responsible for our success. I am so blessed that now I know those superstitions have nothing to do with reality. God is always behind it all. I still remember the beautiful crimson color of this cactus flower. Today I would interpret the bloom as God's love. Red is love. I would not put my trust in mere things, people, and places, but I do put my trust in the most important of all, the One representing immortality and hope; His name is Jesus Christ.

Those cactus plants were the last thing I saw as we were exiting the building, and the image remains as vivid today as it was then. Even now, I recall the dark stairs. We walked very slowly and quietly, not wanting to wake anyone, especially the police informant on our floor. We knew she might wonder why we were leaving at 3:00 a.m. with suitcases and not taking the elevator.

My paternal Aunt Mimi had keys to our home. She was asked by the authorities to empty the apartment immediately because it was being seized. She told me that she was sobbing uncontrollably while clearing out our possessions. We had furniture that was custom made. She also told me that she felt that the furniture reminded her of all of us—our smell, our touch was upon it. She loved us so much and she missed us even more. I assume caressing our belongings for one last time, she felt near to us. Most of her memories of us had been stolen. However, when I returned ten years later, I found my favorite teddy bear being held close by my aunt as she slept. She had hugged him so many times he had become ragged. She held my memory near her heart for a long time. When she held my bear, she saw my hands and my face touching her; my scent was emanating from the stuffed toy. Connection between the two of us began the moment I was born; she did not have children of her own; I was her girl. She shed tears for many years, yearning for her girl to return. This toy represented me; she could release her longing for me through my toy. My cactus plants were blooming at her balcony only to remind her that some day we would meet again. We did. It was a touching moment for both Aunt Mimi and Aunt Ketti when I returned for the first time after ten long years. Although they cried when it was time for me to head home to the States after a vacation, they were excited every time I would return for a visit. I still cry when I think of it all . . . Mimi passed away in 2010. Part of me still wishes I could hear her voice and hug her dearly; Ketti is still alive, thank God. We talk often; she is so grateful and so am I.

It took more than a year before we traveled to Austria. During this time every evening we would gather in front of a short-wave radio and listen to "The Voice of America." This program included discussion about emigration and provided us with valuable details about the process. On occasion, we would listen to BBC and another program called "Freedom Europe." From these programs, we were gathering information of what we could expect beyond the iron curtain.

The long-awaited day arrived; we drove in our automobile to the border, leaving our home in the early hours of the morning. Because my dad did not place the required sticker on the back windshield when we left our apartment, he needed to put it in place at the border. His hand trembled while he made small talk with the border officer. They agreed that when we came back, I would meet his son. This officer was not aware that such promises would never become a reality. We were silently waving our farewells to everyone and everything. The sun came up, but we kept driving; my parents were determined to get as close to the border as possible. We planned to cross the Austrian border the next day to be far enough from eventual forced return. We heard stories that Yugoslavian officials were trading runaways like ourselves for desirable cattle for meat. When we reached Zagreb, a point before crossing the Austrian border, we slept. Very early the next day we were at the border patrol of the Yugoslavian-Austrian border. Once we crossed and saw the first sign in German, we finally exhaled with relief.

When packing my belongings, I remember I decided to wear two pair of pants and four shirts underneath my coat because my tiny suitcase was filled to capacity. A sad memory lingers in my mind when I remember how I tore up a note book filled with my poetry. I knew I would not have space for it in my suitcase so I was reading every poem for one last time, and then tearing the sheet of paper with tears in my eyes knowing this could never be reproduced and will forever be lost in the trash. I filled my pockets with precious memorabilia, chunks of my past. I was clenching my fists just to feel them. It was a cold winter. Sleep deprivation and fear, combined with excitement, kept me shaking.

The trees were passing by. I was half asleep, filled with memories going back and forth in my mind between the present and the past. "Is this a dream, or we really did make it?" I asked myself.

The car was humming monotonously; my mom and dad were silent. The journey we started from southeast had finished somewhere between stamping passports while leaving one country and stamping them back when entering the next. There were so many questions in my mind, begging to come out. I decided to read the signs instead. Tears from sun rays glistening in my eyes, the snow, the wet grass, my breath on the side window, all were so real . . . I was tired but joyous. Getting closer to the capital made me so impatient; I had never experienced a capitalist society where true freedom might be possible. I was absolutely curious—maybe somehow nostalgic, but content. "Will I meet some relatives of grandma here? I need to get my German in order." I was half talking and half thinking.

A new journey was started the moment we crossed the border of the long-awaited Austria, marked with our entrance into Vienna. The first two nights we slept in a very fancy hotel, and then we found reasonable accommodations. We decided to wait a week before we made any decision. A need to save our limited resources was inevitable. We were not going back; we did not know how, where, or how long we needed to survive on the few thousand dollars we had brought with us. Mom knew German, so she was our guide and interpreter. After long walks, sightseeing, and serious talks, we convinced Mama the decision to become an immigrant was insistent.

Ready to cut our ties with the past and open a new page in our future, we contacted a friend of my dad. He had emigrated years earlier. He took us to an immigration camp called Traiskirchen (Three Churches), twenty kilometers from Vienna. The guards placed us under quarantine for a week. We were brought in and not allowed to have contact with the outside world. Each of us was individually interviewed in a room in front of officials who were checking the veracity of our stories. The whole environment was giving me chills; it was quite shocking. It felt as though we were captives or prisoners of war. Nothing prepared us for this: we were nobodies. As we entered the check point, we were asked to surrender our passports. We were illegitimate at the time of our stay. Starting a new life was a painful and scary experience, infused with many unknowns. We had to cross out everything we had known and held dear; we knew we were at a point of no return.

In time we learned that if we had returned exactly one month after our departure, we would not have been imprisoned. But if we had returned later, we would have faced incarceration. This is why my father felt we had to wait until we became American citizens, so we could be protected by the Constitution of the United States. Yes, we were considered enemies of the communist political system at the time. Although I realized this was protocol, the new experiences were frightful…

The tall, massive building was an old army facility; it had bars on the windows. The rooms had bunk beds, wooden tables and chairs, bare floors, and outside bathrooms. We shared a room with another family. The guards gave us metal bowls, spoons, and forks and took us to a cafeteria where we ate. The military environment made me feel worried and uneasy. One week passed very slowly. After that, we were placed in a huge room with many other families, where we slept waiting to be relocated to other parts of the country. To my surprise, we ended up in a pleasant and picturesque village called Illmitz, located in the Federal state of Burgenland, to the east of Lake Neusiedl on the opposite side of Hungary. My father was fearful that we were too close to a communist country; he was saying, "I can see the towers of the border patrol across the lake, and I do not like it." Any reminder of his past was reason to worry; he did not want to relive the horror of his youth. In our documentation, he insisted we state we were not remaining in Austria; we would instead head for the North American continent.

My maternal grandma (Omama) was Austrian, and this fact helped us secure an Austrian asylum. Our choice was different, to travel beyond the Atlantic Ocean many miles away to a safe destination like the United States or Canada. We liked the U.S. In less than ten months, we were scheduled to fly with TWA (Trans World Airlines) to New York City. I was so eager. In the mind of every person, U.S.A. translated into freedom, especially people from the former communist countries.

My mom's father was a lawyer who liked to tell the truth, and his gift of rhetoric took him straight to another barbaric labor camp. He was forced to move wooden trunks on his shoulders from one riverbank to the other. He was practically in the water from sunrise to sundown. From stories I heard, all residents ate water snakes. As for any other "luxuries," the living conditions were not different from the other atrocious camps.

My maternal granddad was one of the fortunate few survivors who lived to see his family. He never spoke of those times; I learned the stories from my mom. While her father was deliberately imprisoned, my mother's daily menu consisted of boiled dry fruits for months and months. Three females: my mom, her sister, and my oma with scarce resources coming from grandma's work at a brick factory, were barely making it. On numerous occasions the family was deported from town to town, blemished for being enemies of the ruling party.

With this background, it was no surprise that we wanted out. On September 17, 1986, we landed at LaGuardia Airport in New York City, and, as dad stepped out, he kneeled and kissed the ground with tears in his eyes. This picture remains in my memory, as though time stood still.

Liberty for many people holds a different meaning, but to my family this word holds something uniquely special. To wake up in the morning and know that there are no recollections of death, no constant reminders of a broken childhood, no fear of imprisonment is a treasure hard to understand unless experienced with the same intensity as my family. Freedom to speak your mind and be protected by the Constitution, freedom to worship God without hiding, freedom to exhale without being tormented is another meaningful prize. Only those who lived through the barbaric communism and felt the bitter consequences know the true meaning of this word. I am not comparing to other people's understanding of freedom; I simply emphasize on our unique experiences. There are many who found meaning in the word –freedom--through their own life encounters.

Wake up, America! Socialism is a prelude to communism; people need to know the bare truth about communism. It is a utopia, false teaching, and a big fat lie that deceives the heart, the soul, and the mind, entangling them in fear. Fear is the tactic radical Marxism uses. Do not confuse communism with Christianity. Communism proclaims: false ideals of equality and redistribution of wealth. Christianity, on the other hand, is teaching equality and giving the means to achieve it. Christianity enlightens people regarding the need to help one another unselfishly. Those are at two ends of the spectrum. One is false; the other is the ultimate truth. Under communism we see: oppression, brutality, rights taken away, forbidden freedoms, and policing the casual resident—all propaganda is oriented to brainwash and dull the senses of the masses. Communism is a dictatorship and despotism; one party remains during the entire rule. Listening, obeying, and agreeing with dogmas that serve the ruling party are imposed. Communism and fascism are both sides of one coin.

Communists try to deceive people by promises of equal opportunities; only Jesus teaches us that if we have two garments, give one to the needy. This is not the case under totalitarianism; the government would take both shirts convincing you, you do not need them. A widely used tactic was imprisonment without a cause to control and infuse fear with one goal in mind to break the individual's spirit.

I remember my younger aunt had a male friend from Western Germany, and he visited us years ago. A patrol car was stationed in front of the building in order to spy on conversations led in the home. He was followed everywhere; the police needed to know his moves and whereabouts. My mom recalls that after he left, the authorities came to confiscate items he had brought and detained us until they identified items not allowed in the country, demanding we surrender all foreign currency he left us. I was only two, so I do not remember all of the details.

My father, while still young, was stationed against his will in labor reserve forces. Only three days had passed since his arrival. He was told he had to work inside uranium mines. He refused to do so. He wanted to have children, knowing people who had worked in those uranium mines for only a year had become sterile and some were diagnosed with cancer. My father was not sworn yet, as every soldier who gets to swear to protect his homeland could not refuse the military orders. If

41

sworn, he would have been sent to military prison. He was arrested, nevertheless, and sent to a labor camp for three years where his daily requirement was unachievable. He was sent to a quarry where everyone was overworked and tortured laboring sixteen, seventeen hours a day. My dad survived this ordeal on water and a piece of bread for his daily meal. He found a neighbor from childhood who had become one of the assault men. He told my father that if he did not scream like he was being killed when beaten, the assault officer will be killed instead. So, my father tried to act the best he could; his life was spared. Years passed before Dad recovered from this savagery.

My childhood was full of love. My dad's sisters adored me. My grandma cherished me. I have precious memories. I am grateful that I lived with Mom and Dad who made sure I was happy. My father had the means to provide for us. I remember my first bike and my sweet puppy. Thank God for all!

Love, friendship, and family could not be stolen by a despotic government; dictators and their subordinates could only steal, hate, separate, and kill. Later, in the pre-abolition era, during Gorbachev's and Reagan's presidencies, life was easier because, to no one's knowledge, a rotten regime was dying. On November 9, 1989, the Berlin wall separating West from East Germany fell to mark the beginning of liberation from oppression. A new era was born that day, one that represented the desire of people for freedom! Those memories bring tears to my eyes; I witnessed great events during my lifetime!

I feel blessed that I had both parents, and together we left behind many sad memories, especially for them. A new beginning gave us hope and helped us dream of a better tomorrow. I am convinced that deep down in his soul my father lived half of his life only to see the dawn of the second half and taste liberty at its best.

In the beginning, our new life was not easy; many components were needed to knit comfort. We needed to learn the language, to dip in the culture, and become part of the melting pot. There were people who took advantage of our inexperience, and there were others whose help proved invaluable. I kept one truth in my heart, and quote it when asked, "If necessary, I would do it again." I was proud of Father's courage and boldness. At fifty-three years of age; he still had the bravery to start over. My mom felt being immigrants was not a life for us. Who can blame her; immigrants are people who often leave only because they have to, not because they want to.

There is this invisible thread that brings us back to the land where it all started, the land where we were born. People we love dearly, friends we left behind, relatives who miss us, and we miss them; they are irreplaceable. It is not enough to just talk on the phone when you wish to have a human touch to embrace and kiss, to look someone in the eye and tell them how much they are loved.

My grandpapa the lawyer died almost five years before I went back, and we never had a chance to say "Goodbye." A letter from him recently became mine. My mom gave it to me with tears in her eyes; it was on my parents' wedding anniversary that Opapa passed away. In his letter he spoke about God and how he longed to see us one more time . . . how his shaky hands did not allow him to hand-write. He used a typewriter. I was searching for a date; there was none, only his signature was meticulously calligraphed and made me cry. The only piece of him left as a reminder; I have no other items to hold dear. What a style this man had—his writing brought emotions to the surface, and I was holding my breath. He was so lonely, so broken. Like every parent, he had doubts about us being well in a distant land among people we did not know. Deep down he loved us so much. "My most dear and beloved children . . ." he begins. "I hope in our dreams God is with us." I never knew this man's knowledge of God. "I hope," he said, "that our desires would not remain unanswered." He called my dad with an endearing name, saying that my father promised to " . . . celebrate Christmas together!?" The question mark tells me he had doubts we would see each other once more. He died almost paralyzed by pain; leftovers from his stay at the death camp.

My father loved playing the guitar. Many times he and Granddad sang beautiful songs while all of us gathered at the table listening and accompanying them.

The letter continued, ". . . again the songs would echo at our desolate, quiet home with the accords of . . ." my dad's guitar, ". . . again we would all sing the endearing song *Two Oaks* with a romantic feeling. With this song C. (Steve) promised to send me into the hereafter." *Two Oaks* was my grandfather's favorite tune. He was extremely sad, pouring his heart and soul on paper: ". . . hope you are not lying to me and I will cease in my hopelessness to sing, *Become Black You Forest . . .*" He ended with, "I hug you with so much warmth and kiss you all three endlessly. Yours."

The letter concluded with his meticulously calligraphed signature.

For my parents' wedding, Opapa (old Papa) handcrafted a beautiful queen-sized bed, where I once jumped and played. Mama liked the comfort of our home. After all, it took a lifetime to turn a house into a home. She made sure we lived cozily and peacefully. Father equipped our apartment with every modern convenience for a tranquil and accommodating existence. But, without a doubt, he was ready and fearless to leave it all behind and fly far from these comforts. Being young and full of energy, I was also ready. We did not emigrate for economic prosperity; we were a classic case of political immigrants. I still keep the *Washington Post* article that was published in the early 1990's by an American reporter who interviewed my aunt Mimi and took photos with my grandmother on the balcony of their apartment.

The roots for executing our plan were embedded into the tragedy of my parents' childhood experiences. Money does not earn emotional and spiritual freedom as some may argue; painful memories remain with us for a lifetime. Broken homes, shattered people, killed individuals cannot be replaced. In the end freedom was the ultimate prize for my dearest parents; they deserved it more than words can express.

Thank you, Jesus!

6

Face-to-Face with Jesus

Then Jesus told him, "Because you have seen me, you have believed; blessed are those who have not seen and yet have believed."
—*John 20:29, NIV*

This is a reminder of the night I was released by my Heavenly Father to fly far above the ocean. Here is the horizon and the beauty of the ocean, the waves, the clouds, the peace… absolutely breathtaking.

More than thirty years ago Jesus became my Lord. As a new baby in Christ, I was daring and hungry for knowledge; my desire to see amazing things grew exponentially.

After reading how Jesus had called individuals in the middle of the night and had taken them to heaven to personally show them the wonders of the sky, I started to desire this experience. A dear friend told me how Christ sat on the couch, and they both had a meaningful conversation. I started praying for the same thing; my prayer was simple and honest. I asked God to come and meet me but be gentle and not scare me. Six months passed and nothing happened, yet my faith was not shaken. The more I waited, the more I wanted it.

One ordinary afternoon I went to my bedroom, with the intention to lie down for a few minutes to gather my thoughts. It was sunny outside and so quiet around me. I had covered my bed neatly, so I sat on the edge just emptying my mind from the stress of the day. Then, slowly I placed my head on the pillow. Not a minute passed, and I rested my eyelids but did not fall asleep. I suddenly became airborne. I was flying upwards with the speed of light, like a bullet tearing the air. I kept flying up, and deeper into the vast sky expanse, and the further I flew the more interesting my flight had become. Oh, it was so exhilarating; my head was ripping the invisible surroundings! I felt light as a feather and very courageous. After the earth's atmosphere finished, I entered the black vacuum where I flew just as fast as before, feeling absolutely free. Finally, I reached a flat surface--it was white and shiny. There was light everywhere but not from the sun; the Bible tells us that God is the light up there. Revelation talks about it, "There will be no more night. They will not need the light of a lamp or the light of the sun, for the Lord God will give them light." (Revelation 22:5a, NIV) Our sun was created by God on day four. It gives light unto planets in the solar system. Heaven is beyond the solar system and all the other galaxies that are in the second heaven. Flying upwards until I reached a destination called the third heaven, my flight ceased. I placed my elbows on top of the new surface, and I rested my chin onto my hands, surprised to discover that actually heaven is not round. My body was freely dangling into the boundless territory underneath, and, even then, I felt no fear from falling. In spirit we do not know fear; the spirit in us is the Holy Spirit, one of the persons from the triune nature of God—God-Father-Yahweh, God-Son-Jesus Christ, and God-the Holy Spirit.

This moment was the pinnacle of my journey; before my very eyes I saw something extraordinary. Two huge sliding doors opened, and a figure that emanated almost blinding light started coming towards me. Right then and there, I knew it was Jesus Christ. His clothing was whiter than any white I have ever seen. Pure white was infused with light, creating an incomprehensible coalescence; it was breathtaking! This experience reminds me of the transfiguration of Jesus before the disciples in (Matthew 17:2, NLT), "As the men watched, Jesus' appearance was transformed so that his face shone like the sun, and his clothes became as white as light." My eyes were wide open. I have never seen such astonishing beauty! I was speechless. I remained in awe and quite motionless as though time stood still. I wanted to just remain there, but my time was limited--ordained by God. Only those who pass away may remain in the presence of the Lord. It is my belief that Jesus allowed this experience for witnessing purposes. Torn between reality and the supernatural, I found myself flying back towards home. It was quite fast, and when I reached my body, I entered it by both inhaling and exhaling. Wow! Did I see myself lying on the bed? Absolutely; I knew it was not a dream. This was unexplainable by the laws of nature, beyond any scientific proof. I had no doubt the experience was an answer to my prayer. Before my flight, I remember emphatically—I put my head on the pillow, and I turned towards the clock on my right. I noticed the time was exactly 4:00 p.m. When my spirit came back from heaven, and plunged into my body, I saw the time again. It was 4:20 p.m. I believe it was not a coincidence that I looked at the clock twice; God wanted me to notice the elapsed time. In essence, I realized that heaven is just minutes away from earth if we fly with the speed of light. I am convinced that when my time comes to say goodbye to the world, I will repeat this experience in my spiritual form. I would feel just as good as I felt at that incredible moment.

Fully aware that Jesus exists and perceiving the reality of heaven was the most remarkable experience of my life. I asked myself, "Did I just saw Christ? What just happened and why was I chosen?" Is it because I was expected to tell the world about it? It could just be that. God wants everyone to know that there are eyewitnesses who saw Him, and even communicated with Him. God also wants to assure the doubting Thomases that He is alive, and well, and so real.

I have a reverential respect for my Lord, not only because I saw Him--it certainly helps—but for all the love He has bestowed upon me. In the midst of tragic moments, He sends me a heavenly peace. He has this ability to turn a frown into a smile. Best Friend, incredible Father, He can be whatever we need Him to be, and He does it perfectly. My life is rich because of Him. Much of my character has been improved in a positive way due to God's most gentle and kind method for correcting it. I have found meaning in the unimportant things, for He shows me what matters most. Every aspect of our lives is important in the eyes of the Lord. He also looks from the inside out, while we look from the outside in. In (1 Samuel 16:7, NLT), "The Lord doesn't see things the way we see them. People judge by outward appearances, but the Lord looks at the heart."

God taught me wisely to accept and love myself. Loneliness used to bother me a lot, but Jesus assured me that I am never alone, and I should not be anxious when there is quietness. I choose to enjoy the peace, to do my daydreaming, and relax. Stress can be very damaging, so "me time" with Jesus can reduce stress. If ever my fear gets the upper hand, Jesus delicately calms me down, and His compassion brings placid resolution. (2 Timothy 1:7, KJV) states, "For God hath not given us the spirit of fear; but of power, and of love, and of a sound mind."

When I take a break and sit down I often look at the sky. Ever wondered how birds fly? I did many times, and, one amazing moment, I had the opportunity to find out exactly how birds feel. I asked my Heavenly Father to show me. You see, Jesus Christ answered my prayers in a very accurate manner, nothing more or nothing less than what I've requested. Several years ago, in the middle of the night, somewhere between two and four a.m., I found myself soaring towards the ocean. I flew far and deep above the ocean immensity. My town borders the Atlantic Ocean, and that night I flew in a familiar territory. I looked down, and I saw the beach I have visited many times. It felt so elating, so pleasant; I turned back toward the shore, and I saw familiar surroundings. I flew above the pier, and I was fearless again. Everything around me was peaceful and calm; only the ocean waves were caressing the sand shore gently. The Earth beneath me was sleeping, but I was wide awake and very excited to fly and fly and fly. There, at the place where ocean and sand meet, I turned my head north, and I noticed tall buildings, where all of the windows were dark. Every soul was asleep. I lost track of time, but it was still very early when I came back into my body. My spirit entered back, and this time the feeling reminded me of my past encounter. For the second time in my life, I had an out of body experience. "So this is how birds fly!?" I said to myself. Such an exuberating moment! So much joy and freedom I felt while in flight!

A week later we were walking on the pier. Incidentally, I turned my head in the direction of the tall buildings and I was reminded of my flight. I told my husband, "Honey, I flew last week here in the middle of the night . . ." The buildings were bathing in sunlight. My husband must have been daydreaming. He remained silent as though my words rushed away with the wind . . . In these moments, I feel as though all supernatural experiences can only be understood by my Lord and me. It is not easy to interpret for others every emotion and sensation felt. English, being such a rich language, still does not have terminology for everything that exists in the spiritual realm. Be assured we will know one day. Until then, let us remain trusting.

While at the pier, I closed my eyes, thinking about two things. First, I noticed a vast difference in sensations—one being within my body (I had more controlled and acute perception but many limitations) and the other when in spirit (There was no obstruction of any kind; the weightlessness evoked freedom, effortless movements, absolute peace, and not a care in the world). When in spirit, negative emotions lacked, because in spirit we are going to last forever, but also our spirit is part of God's Spirit where only positive emotions exist; He made sure we are no longer subject to matter, or time but subject to the Spirit of God. Sadness and stress affect the body and its vitality. We should hold on to positive emotions as long as we could to help our bodies' longevity regardless of the fact that our bodies come from dust, and they shall return to dust as the Bible tells us. Our bodies are a temporary shell for a temporary life . . .

I loved flying, and later I prayed for the same experience to repeat. I am so grateful that it happened because it was all worth it. I certainly trust that the future holds many more surprises so I remain hopeful.

I pondered over what would have happened if my husband had found me at that moment lying in bed. Wouldn't he have been shocked that I was motionless and silent? Or did I still breathe even though my spirit was outside? I have no answer yet, but God most likely would not have left my body to deteriorate.

Miracles happen in all shapes and sizes. They provide us with answered prayers, healings, and new life. Ceasing poverty, bondage breaking, and mental restorations are all miraculous. I am left with the belief that every cell in my body received new information, and my emotions were amplified because of both flights. As a result, there is a renewal, closeness, and deepened relationship with my Lord!

Isn't this the essence of our faith . . .?

7

Miracles of Great Importance

Most certainly I tell you, he who believes in me, the works that I do, he will do also; and he will do greater works than these, because I am going to my Father. Whatever you will ask in my name, I will do it, that the Father may be glorified in the Son. If you will ask anything in my name, I will do it.
—John 14:12-14, WEB

My daughter sitting on the special chair God graced us with. This is a brand new rocking chair with soft, pink cushions, exactly what I was dreaming of. Faith bigger than a mustard seed can bring something extraordinary. Thank you Lord for the perfect gift!

My daughter was born in the dawn of the millennium. My husband was joking that if she were born in the first second of the year 2000, she would be famous. I distinctly remember a story by Asia-Pacific/BBC News about the firstborn of the millennium: Fiji's first millennium birth, a boy born at 0018 local time (1118 GMT): mom and baby were featured in the newspapers, on TV, magazines and everywhere.

We welcomed her with open arms; she was our miracle, a heavenly gift, and a long-awaited joy. I prayed for her long before I was married. One day I recall speaking to her as though she were there, although I did not know the gender then.

So perfect and so ready to take on the world; she was a very peaceful and quiet baby, sleeping all night, crying very little and smiling all the time. Every morning, as I was approaching her crib, the world would lit up. I had a purpose to smile. Unlike other moms, my sleep was not interrupted. There were no midnight feedings, walking back and forth until the baby calms down. My tiny bundle was an absolute perfection, yet the doctors were concerned that she was not eating during the night. My husband was convinced that we had it great—why fix something that was not broken?

During the pregnancy, by doctor's recommendation, I rested and had time to indulge in reading. There was no stress; my days were surrounded by calmness, great books, dreaming and planning for my baby and certainly healthy foods. After Victoria's birth, my first appointment at the gynecologist was due. I asked my husband to join me that day. After the doctor completed a routine exam, he looked concerned and performed an ultrasound. He also took pictures of my cervix I did not ask why, but still wondered about it. I waited on the examining table while he went outside; it seemed like forever. The room was small and there were no windows, I felt squeezed between the four walls. Many thoughts crossed my mind. He came back and told me to join him at his office with my husband. While I was getting dressed, I felt weak in the knees. I was beyond myself, and the whole room was spinning slowly. I did not want to hear whatever news he had. I wished I could put my hands over my ears and block his voice. As he was placing the enlarged negatives on a lighted screen, I almost cried… the doctor pointed to an area that indicated abnormality. I was not ready for the shocking news. According to him the tissue in question suggested precancerous cells. My heart sank. We set a follow up appointment in a week to discuss a further plan of action.

Tears were warming my cheeks. Walking reluctantly, I embraced my husband's arm, and the hallway seemed so long and narrow. I needed to leave this building as soon as possible, and breathe the outside air. At the parking lot, Will stopped, tenderly took my hands, and in his eyes I saw deep love. "Do not worry," he said. "I am with you; we will beat this I promise." I cried silently all the way home thinking, "No, Lord, please. You know I want a second child." My thoughts were racing between the news and my earnest desire to have more children. "What now? How would I talk about it?" I was crushed. Gradually somewhere between the driveway and the house, God very gently dried up my face, and I felt overtaken by a supernatural peace. "Peace I leave with you; my peace I give you. I do not give to you as the world gives. Do not let your hearts be troubled and do not be afraid" (John14:27, NIV).

This was the turning point; I was no longer afraid but certain that God was going to heal me. My cry turned into strength, my pessimism into hope and I was assured that God would bring healing into completion. I started praying fervently every day, and my faith grew immensely. I was confident that God's promises would prevail; the Holy Spirit infused me with trust and I felt strong and secure. I remembered boldly that Jesus took my sickness on the cross two thousand years ago.

My next appointment was full of anticipation, as I was sitting at the doctor's office convinced of absolute victory. After the exam I heard him saying, "You are in remission." He took more pictures and he examined them carefully; the proof was in his hands. Hooray! I was ready to jump off the chair. I had already informed my husband that I expected a positive outcome. I told the doctor that it was all God's doing; whether he believed me, I couldn't be certain. In Jeremiah chapter 30 verse 17 the Lord promises exactly this, "For I will restore health to you and heal you of your wounds." (Jeremiah 30:17a, NKJV)

I wanted my husband to be encouraged by this great news. He didn't share his feelings; he wanted to stay strong for my sake, but

I knew he was worried about my life. I was rejoicing. William was peaceful. The doctor had no medical explanation except that, in his professional opinion, "The body can heal itself." This might be true, but I knew different, "Nothing is impossible for God" as (Luke 1:37) declares.

That day I felt like reaching new horizons. Not long after that, another great miracle added to my list. A prophetic word was given by a Christ follower; he spoke of a "snake" in my stomach. Spiritually translated the revelation meant that there was a spirit of pain tormenting my body. Usually chronic diseases are believed to be of supernal nature as well as physical. About three years before I married Will, I used to have episodes of debilitating pain in my stomach associated with a lot of vomiting and fever. Several doctors later, the root of the problem was still unknown. One Sunday afternoon I had the same symptoms, and my husband drove me to the emergency room. The next day I was on the operating table, for I was diagnosed with chronic appendicitis. The surgeon explained that while the crisis occurred, I had the symptoms; but, as soon as the prodromes subsided, my appendix was acting normal. After the surgery only the memory of it remained. What a relief! I was recovering and thanking God for healing me.

Some individuals claim and insist that miracles do not exist. Others like the cessationalists are certain that they existed only in Biblical times, believing they are a thing of the past. In my opinion the miraculous age is still in effect today as much as it was during Biblical times. God does not change things that define Him just because we live in the twenty-first century. He is the same yesterday, as well as today and tomorrow. "Jesus Christ the same yesterday, and today, and forever." (Hebrews 13:8, KJV).

I still see supernatural activities because I have encountered them directly and personally.

Nature lover as I am, afternoon walks are a treat for me. Last week, the sun was warming my face; the birds were chirping sweetly; life was exploding all around me, and the air was filled with flowers' unique perfumes. Close your eyes and imagine it. Life as we know it is in fact miraculous—every flower with its vibrant colors, playful squirrels nestling within the trees, Blue Jays and Northern Cardinals, rich green blades of grass, every cloud—cumulus or cirrostratus. I realized as I was walking that all the things I have grown accustomed to—things I think of as ordinary—are in fact extraordinary. How didn't I see it before?

Ordinary is miraculous, just like the extraordinary. Today my perception of the supernatural has extended into all that surrounds me. I realize that my senses have been dulled by looking at actual miracles all the time. Every creation is amazing—humans, fish, animals (domestic and wild), nature in every shape and form.

Earth and everything in it, regardless of how simple it may seem at first glance. The stars and the seemingly endless cosmos with all planets, galaxies, black holes, red giant stars, and celestial satellites—these are all examples of God's miraculous creation that we see every night. Did you know that every star has its own unique sound and when combined with the sounds of the other stars can produce a symphony? Recently, scientists have explored more in-depth the sounds of planets. I watched an impressive video on You Tube where scientists captured those sounds of planets and stars. Similarly, Louis Giglio shared the symphony of whales and stars (Giglio, 2011). When I heard the music and saw the video of the absolutely breathtaking images, I could not get my eyes off of it.

Because I get excited by God's deeds and have been experiencing supernatural phenomenon, I believe it all. Do you believe in miracles? I do! I see them bombarding us everywhere, if only we can open our spiritual eyes and believe the impossible.

This afternoon stroll reminded me of one of these joyful moments years back. I trusted; I acted upon my belief; and I received more than I could possibly imagine. I received an item that I still love and my daughter uses.

My life was interesting from the very beginning, and when it flew like an invisible spirit over the waters of time, I reached a point of receiving supernaturally. This time of acquiring started when my daughter was a tiny toddler. The small apartment, walking distance from the ocean, was nestled among a parking lot and a tranquil backyard. Beneath us, lived a family of four—a husband, wife, and two children. The lady mentioned one day that if I needed anything for my baby, I could call a Catholic charity. I had many things, but, out of curiosity, I picked up the phone and dialed. Located to the north, I drove to see the benevolence organization; it was a small building with two scaled-down rooms. I decided to get a toy or two, figuring I will wash them at home and let my girl play with them. A young female behind the counter told me that if I needed anything else, I could come back. She also added that they appreciated when the people who received would later donate something of their own. This is how they were keeping the charity operational. *Good idea,* I thought to myself. *They need to receive, so they can bless others in need.*

Charity, receiving, it all adds up. It is all in the Bible. It was beautiful to feel the hand of God. This hand gives unconditionally, using people and circumstances. It also opens doors for even bigger blessings. Time had passed since I had visited the charity, and I kept praying. My faith was growing, like a mushroom after refreshing rain. My trust was deepening; I was receiving wisdom, and my character was being shaped in a way I never knew before. A verse came to mind one beautiful day that those who do believe without seeing are blessed (cf: John 20:29). I was prompted to see how it works, and my heart was filled with desire to experience something more than just everyday life. I was at the verge of a big breakthrough. Boom, I picked up the phone and called the Catholic charity. "Hi," I said. "How are you? I have a question. Do you ever receive any furniture besides toys and clothing?" "No," the young voice responded. "We have a limited space, and we have no place to store large items."

Embarrassment and shyness are a part of my nature, but those do not exist when God puts words into my mouth. Boldness and security are prevalent, and I feel I can say or ask anything: "I see, because God told me that you will receive a white rocking chair with pink cushions. I will call you in a week to check, and you will tell me that you have it." Wow! I was stunned, but mostly thinking, *What would she say? Would she decide I was crazy?* . . . Feeling like Moses, I acted bravely. In the past I wanted to buy a white chair with pink cushions. This was a dream but not a necessity. Having a baby made it essential. I was anxious to witness, but patient to wait. A week or so had passed and I called again. My heart was racing, and my hands were shaking, "Hello. Do you remember me? I called a week ago to ask about furniture and tell you about a rocking chair . . ." Meanwhile, I was thinking, *When did I become so courageous?* She did not let me finish. "Oh yes, I remember you!" A pause, "We received two brand new white rocking chairs. An older woman donated them this morning. She said she does not need them, so they are here for you to come and pick them up."

Ah, did I hear correctly!!! Time stopped abruptly; shocked I was and even speechless. This was not my reality it was God's reality. It took me few seconds to shake off the shock and then I was smiling, raising my hands in the air grateful for that news, and I said to her, "I told you, you would receive furniture." She remained silent, possibly not knowing how to respond. My legs were trembling under the table. My heart was beating faster again. I added, "I do not need two; I would only take one." Someone else was going to be blessed with the second chair. I placed the handset on its base and buried my head in my hands. I needed a few moments to grasp the situation and have time to come to terms with a reality that had never touched me before. It is strange to become a participant in something so heavenly amazing, "Thank you, Lord." I whispered. "You are a God of miracles."

I picked Victoria up placed her in the car seat and drove to see my gift from paradise. There they were in the middle of the room standing beautifully—two smooth, wooden, white rocking chairs, crafted so meticulously with light, puffy, pink cushions. Having the tags on them, they were fresh from the store. I could smell the newness. I thanked the girl one more time; then I took both armrests and lifted one of the chairs over my head. The Infinity trunk didn't seem large enough, yet somehow I managed to get the rocking chair inside. After securing the cargo, I headed home to enjoy it.

Never mind how I arrived home, I was driving slowly, but it felt like I was flying. This chair was a priceless treasure. Placing it in front of the TV set, I sat on it for the very first time. From this day onward, Victoria and I were using the spot to rock, to take naps, to sing, read and watch baby programs. My girl was sleeping in the cradle God prepared for her; I was sitting in the midst of a heavenly proof that the promises in the Word are as real as that very rocker. Believe the unbelievable; this gorgeous, shiny rocking chair is still my prized possession.

Almost seventeen years have passed, and I have no intention to separate with it. It is now gracing my young daugher's room. Time passed, so I removed the tag; but, in my heart, this is not just any chair. It is an invaluable jewel. This furniture piece is a heirloom that hopefully will remain in the family for generations. I was given a perfect rocking chair just as I had envisioned it.

In the beginning while still a baby in the faith, I had amazing opportunities to witness so many miracles! Our backyard was full of trees and vegetation and so many cute and bright-colored exotic birds. It looked like paradise; I loved it. God spoke to me one night, calling me. I was sleeping peacefully, and I heard the voice of God. I woke up and went to the balcony, convinced I had to gather the dry laundry. Since I did not have a place for a dryer, I had clothes' lines below the balcony railing. Like Samuel, I was called; but there was no Eli to tell me who called. I went on the balcony, and suddenly I was in the midst of an energized cloud that was buzzing with light and electrical charge. I was paralyzed. I could not move or speak. I was not scared, as much as amazed. I was standing on sacred ground, in a cloud of glory without knowing it. God called me by my first name. He also told me something very significant, "Your prayer will be answered." Time stopped, and I forgot to ask, "Which one?" The cloud was gone and so was my God. My first afterthought was *He does not use nicknames.* Then, I was puzzled which prayer, but He never revealed exactly which one; so every answered prayer for me is "the one." Sometimes I still wonder if He meant a specific prayer. Either way, I will cherish this spiritual explosion.

My adventures did not cease. God continues to give, speak, heal, and surprise me by making and delivering more promises. Who knows? Maybe I have more pages to fill. I am leaving it in His hands to lead me and guide me. I remain faithful and lean on Jesus Christ who is my solid rock. For in His name, it all started; and in His name, it will all continue.

Epilogue

Then God said, "Let us make mankind in our image, in our likeness, so that they may rule over the fish in the sea and the birds in the sky, over the livestock and all the wild animals, and over all the creatures that move along the ground."
—Genesis 1:26, NIV

I was so emotional during the writing of this book. I had an insatiable desire to write- meaning in Latin / Cacoethes Scribendi/. It took days and nights to finish it in between eye injury and all. I listened to Will and took a day off, but my heart was anxious to finish and bring it all to life. This book contains the nuts and bolts of my life. Those pages reveal so many details about my family and truths of how I feel. My past, how I came here, my roots, and my future are embedded in it. My deepest emotions, my divine encounters, my tears, and every feeling that I experienced is on the pages of this material. I did not take this task lightly; I poured my heart into it because I believe that people need to know the hard truth. People need to hear and understand what communism is and what might be if they allow this atrocious regime to overtake our beloved America, the country where I came thirty some years ago and today I call home. I also believe they ought to hear how God heals emotionally and physically--how He saw me through many harsh moments. God shines above all earthly temptations and we are capable to overcome everything when walking beside Him and succumb to His guidance. I am alive, and I am all God's. We are all His, created in His impressive image.

On the first day of creation, God said, "Let there be light," and the light instantly overcame the darkness (Genesis 1:3, NIV). Ephesians 1:5 discusses how we were chosen in the Lord before the foundation of the earth. Much like the light coming to existence, our creation was almost instantaneous. The first man was created from dust; God "breathed into his nostrils" and then put him to sleep, so the first woman could be created (Genesis 2:7, NIV). All happened in less than a day. According to science, it can take from thirty minutes to seventy-two hours for each of us to be conceived. This is also an instant happening compared to eternity. In essence all things God created here on earth are done in a short period of time, and done in such perfection only a perfect God is capable of this kind of excellence. I strongly believe that the notion of time does not exist in heaven; eternity can't harbor time since in this word there is no beginning and end, it simply continues forever.

The Bible interestingly compares us to the light: in the words of Jesus, we are "the light of the world." (Matthew 5:14, WEB) Without a doubt we are here for a divine reason and with a great purpose. Let us act accordingly by being positive examples, righteous leaders, and humble followers of the one true God.

Accountability is a part of it. It translates into conscious pursuit. Is it achievable to copy a sinless Being? We can come close . . . It takes discipline and motivation, and then accomplishment comes. I have tried and failed but did not give up and finally tried and succeeded. The latter brought me immeasurable satisfaction. Doing it right in the face of worldly pressure and temptations is a daily commitment, not without a price. Weary and tired, it is easy to lose interest, but shall we conform to this world? If the answer is "No.", then we ought to stop. As God teaches us in Romans 12 verse 2, "Do not conform to the pattern of this world, but be transformed by the renewing of your mind. Then you will be able to test and approve what God's will is—his good, pleasing and perfect will." we need to listen. (NIV) We shall keep on plugging our lives to the invisible lifeline coming from heaven and get supernaturally imbued. Then we can experience the truth in verse 33 from John 16, "I have told you these things, so that in me you may have peace. In this world you will have trouble. But take heart! I have overcome the world." (NIV) What better way than to have a daily reading of the greatest book of all times called Bible. I have no doubt we need a daily dose of J.C. We also need to rest in Him in order to get ready for the next chapter in our lives. God rested after Creation. He is God and we are mere mortals. We need days of complete surrender for spiritual and physical renewal.

Life on Earth will one day be like heaven, and God will overcome evil with good but now the prince of darkness makes sure to create confusion. In our quest for better existence, we experience many trials. How do we cope with it? -- is the colossal question. I have only one answer: the faith in Jesus Christ.

Halting to rest is basic; we need also to shift our gaze upon prayer.

God advises us to stay in prayer at all times and in all situations. (cf: Ephesians 6:18) Many times, our prayers should not be for the situation but in the midst of it, trusting Him when it hurts the most. Who can bear our burdens, soften our hearts, and open our minds so we can see the answer clearly? Who better than Him who is the beginner of all things?

Some may ask what is the reason for everything under the sun, and what are we doing here? According to the Bible, we serve a purpose bigger than us, not only for God's divine plan, but for our own salvation. We are the most amazing miracle of all creation, the culmination point! It is genius! It is a reason for pride and happiness. But pride can be deceiving used against us by the king of lies. There is a fine line between humble pride and pride that turns into boasting, climaxing in ego. With this in mind, let us prevent pride from overtaking us. How deceptive it is to believe that we are in control of everything happening to us. Is it we who secure our future, ultimately denying God's indisputable contribution? Proverbs clearly states God's involvement, "The heart of a man plans his way, but the Lord establishes his steps." (Proverbs 16:9, ESV). Chaos and confusion, anxiousness, and arguments are the result of pride and denial.

As children of an omnipotent Triune God, we are here to also serve one another, not as slaves, but as loving brothers and sisters. We are God's first and foremost, and, since initiated from Adam and Eve, we are one big family. Nothing can separate us from God's love, and this love conquers all barriers, so we are all united from the four corners of the world before the throne of our righteous King.

Servitude keeps us in place helps us be humbled, defining even further our purpose here. And my purpose extends from being a long-awaited baby, child, young adult, and woman, into a mom, wife, Bible teacher and writer—all good grounds for a sense of belonging. We all have amazing purposes to be here as part of God's family, which makes life worth living.

It is not that we can control the future, but that we are allowed to make choices.

Making choices is under free will's jurisdiction. We could choose to do wrong, and we could choose to do right. We could choose to be in the middle of the battlefield where the action is. Do not allow life to pass you by. Regrets are born from passiveness. It is as though you never lived . . . So take a chance and do something good, you most certainly would not regret it.

Unfortunate situations exist with or without action on our part. Should we focus on them? Wouldn't we rather rejoice and be glad? Psalm 118 verse 24 urges us to be focused on this day of joy and happiness, especially when the Lord has chosen it for us, "This is the day the Lord has made; We will rejoice and be glad in it." (Psalm 118:24, NKJV) I have a deep desire to feel free from the chains of the "inevitable." My time to dance is now. I had my share of sadness. For every "No" there is a "Yes," and for everything negative there is a positive under the sun. God's plans, regardless of satan's, are always intended for success. The plans God has for us are"...to prosper you(us) and not to harm you(us)... to give you(us) a hope and a future" (Jeremiah 29:11, NIV).

We can pray and trust Jesus Christ serving Him with all our heart— one of the New Testament's commandments.

Heaven will be on Earth one day. Actually, it was like that in the Garden of Eden from Genesis, but our great, great, grandparents Adam and Eve disobeyed and caused all of us to fall victims to sin. So I am restraining myself to jump ahead, there is a lot more yet to be fulfilled, because we still have pages in the bible that are our future and the second coming of our Lord is yet to happen. Heaven still remains at its place, and earth is where God intended it to be. When God created man He gave him dominion over the living things and the land while in the Garden of Eden. The woman, followed by her man disobeyed God's request to not eat from the apple tree. She was deceived by Lucifer (Day Star), and together male and female lost their privileges . . . earning knowledge of good and bad. Look what that brought us.

What do we do when we disobey and sin, and fall short of the glory of God? First, we shall learn not to do it again. Then, ask for forgiveness; and since God is a merciful Father, He forgives—not once, but seventy times seven. We shall continue to better ourselves as long as we live, so one day we will receive crowns in heaven. Until then, I am certain that from a tragedy, a rose could be born. From sadness, a smile comes forth.

At the end, I chose to stop living in the past, no longer worrying and wishing for different, not dwelling on past mistakes and wrong choices.

I pick to remain in the present and hope for the future. God opens our spiritual eyes to see that there are no God's coincidences, only God's incidences.

Whether teaching us a lesson or using us as an example, we shall be open to discipline. Our consciousness is the voice of the Lord. We need to learn compassion and refrain from judging. "Do not judge, or you too will be judged" (Mathew 7:1, NIV).

How could we understand other people's sadness and be kindhearted if we never felt pain, experienced loss, or lived through what they have been through?

I choose to be looking up for my answers and keep calm as much as possible in the face of adversity. I choose to live with optimism.

When sadness overtakes me, I opt to analyze who wants me in the pit. I then choose wisely to listen to the voice of reason and make clever decisions, to step back and give priority to the most important task for the moment, to invite order in the day. In doing this we start to enjoy people we love and begin to appreciate them more. Loving, helping, not missing on moments that would never return, I am appreciating life with the understanding that tomorrow is never promised. I can smell the roses today and wake up the next morning to hear my husband's slow breathing and thank God for him. I can do the same for my daughter, find time to listen, help, and offer advice. I choose to take time and not rush, so I can live my life and be present for it. I also strive to be the best role model I can be. This may sound pretentious, and some may argue that it's easier said than done. I agree. Yet, it is achievable through God's guidance and Biblical advice and our intentional choice. Living our lives intentionally sends a message to the future that we desire to come closer to You—The Alpha and Omega, the Almighty, loving, and precious Father of all mankind.

When close to You, we can ultimately love " . . . with actions and in truth" (1 John 3:18, NIV).

I choose my attitude.

The rest is in the hands of my Creator. He is my Shepherd from (Psalm 23). If we all live such that we can help those around us we will smile more often, and the world can become more beautiful. Change comes softly; it comes when we do not see it. A true effort for a positive change is rewarding. When I fail, I ask for forgiveness first from God, then from others.

There is a truth that is bigger than life, that I can do all through the one and only I praise and bow before. His powerful name is Jesus. I trust "I can do all through Him" because He gives me strength (Philippians 4:13, NIV). Even if I make a mistake, He shields me from falling captive. Christ brings me back to Himself. In the most amazing book ever written, Papa gave me His word, and He keeps His promises because He is the same yesterday, today, and tomorrow. In the tiny details of our lives, there is still reason for us to be. All we have to do is see it, experience it, and appreciate it.

Walking the trail of memories I feel humbled and blessed to have experienced such an amazingly rich life. Thank you for letting me do it all by your side, Daddy. You were present for every up and every down, for every smile and every tear. Your blood had covered it all; this is why it is an honor to be called your daughter, Lord!

One day, when we go to heaven, life on earth will continue without us, and others will walk on our path. They will fulfill what is in store for them.

Shall we use life for something positive? Yes. Shall we cry and be victimized? Best not to.

Choose to make a difference in this world, and then step back and see whether it was worth it. Yes, my friend, last night I really cried when my daughter's friend passed by the house while Vicky was at youth group. I read part of the book to this special girl, and she kept asking questions afterwards, in disbelief that so much pain can exist.

After she left I questioned myself—was the story strong enough to convey the message? Was it written well to tell the truth passionately?

Only time and other readers would be able to answer this question. The bottom line is I obeyed God to sit and write. This is my honorable duty, and I did it with passion and love and deep desire to touch hearts and change lives as a result, all in the honor of God!

In Romans 8:28 we read, "And we know that all things work together for good to them that love God, to them who are called according to his purpose." (AKJV)

About Elizabeth J. Shaw.

"Your greatest message will be spoken by your life NOT your lips."
—*Steven Furtick*

Elizabeth J. Shaw grew up in a small, picturesque European country. She attended the National School of Music and planned to become a professional opera singer. Her unique voice was compared to the voice of one of the most renowned and influential opera singers of the 20th century, Maria Callas.

Elizabeth emigrated to the U.S.A. with her parents in 1986. She attended three colleges. Her early education was in pharmaceutical sciences; however, she did not feel called to pursue this career. Her degree in nutrition helped her gain valuable experience in the field. Working in two hospitals, she also became a nutrition educator in a detention center for young adults and a health club nutrition consultant/lecturer.

Mom and wife, she had the opportunity to home school her daughter. Meanwhile, she was an instructor for more than six years in the public school system. Thirty amazing years with the Lord brought rich experiences and material for this book.

For seventeen years, her calling as teacher and director of a Biblical school proved invaluable to her passion for bringing the Good News to children of all ages. It was centered around one goal: to further the kingdom of God. Ten years ago, she felt a special vocation to put thoughts into words. Finally, this moment was chosen by God himself. Today the author lives on the banks of a scenic lake with amazing sunsets and diverse wildlife. Her cute dog brings joy and laughter to the family. Elizabeth, her husband Will, and her daughter Victoria travel every year, exploring the country and Europe.

Her biggest achievement and highest honorary degree is the one God himself will bestow upon her the day she meets Him again!

Hope you enjoyed reading.

Printed in the United States
By Bookmasters